HUMAN-TO-HUMAN SELLING

HUMAN
TO
HUMAN
SELLING

How to Sell Real and Lasting Value in an
Increasingly Fast-Paced and Digital World

ADRIAN DAVIS

NEW YORK

HUMAN-TO-HUMAN SELLING
How to Sell Real and Lasting Value in an
Increasingly Fast-Paced and Digital World

Published in New York, New York, by Morgan James Publishing. Morgan James and The Entrepreneurial Publisher are trademarks of Morgan James, LLC.
www.MorganJamesPublishing.com

The Morgan James Speakers Group can bring authors to your live event. For more information or to book an event visit The Morgan James Speakers Group at www.TheMorganJamesSpeakersGroup.com.

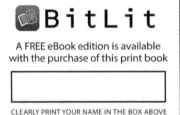

A FREE eBook edition is available
with the purchase of this print book

CLEARLY PRINT YOUR NAME IN THE BOX ABOVE

Instructions to claim your free eBook edition:
1. Download the BitLit app for Android or iOS
2. Write your name in UPPER CASE in the box
3. Use the BitLit app to submit a photo
4. Download your eBook to any device

ISBN 978-1-61448-540-7 paperback
ISBN 978-1-61448-541-4 eBook
ISBN 978-1-61448-542-1 audio
ISBN 978-1-63047-195-8 hardcover
Library of Congress Control Number:
2013941926

Cover Design by:
Chris Treccani
www.3dogdesign.net

Interior Design by:
Bonnie Bushman
bonnie@caboodlegraphics.com

In an effort to support local communities, raise awareness and funds, Morgan James Publishing donates a percentage of all book sales for the life of each book to Habitat for Humanity Peninsula and Greater Williamsburg.

Get involved today, visit
www.MorganJamesBuilds.com

Habitat
for Humanity®
Peninsula and
Greater Williamsburg
Building Partner

To my lovely wife, my trusted advisor and partner.

*To my mother, who has been an ongoing
source of inspiration and strength to me.*

*And to salespeople everywhere who see their
work as a meaningful contribution and a
way of improving the lives of others.*

CONTENTS

ACKNOWLEDGMENTS

I am deeply indebted to the many thought leaders that have influenced my thinking over the many years I have been in sales. These include but are not limited to Zig Ziglar, Les Brown, Michael Gerber, David Maister, Roger Fisher, William Ury, Adrian Slywotzky, Frederick Reichheld, Seth Godin, Neil Rackham, Andrew Sobel, Malcolm Gladwell, Michel Robert, and Kenneth Blanchard.

I would like to express my heartfelt thanks to Cameron Hay, Michelle Davidson, Don Peppers, Martha Rogers, Ph. D., and Randall Craig for their detailed feedback on my manuscript. Thank you for your wisdom and insights. I also want to thank Randall for the time I could spend at his cottage to do four days of focused, uninterrupted writing.

Thanks also to everyone at Morgan James Publishing, whose encouragement and expertise have allowed me to share my message with a wider audience.

I also deeply appreciate my many clients over the years. Thank you for your commitment to your clients and for the privilege of working with you.

Finally, I'm indebted to my lovely wife, Jennifer, for her patience and support. I could never have done this without her.

INTRODUCTION

You don't get in life what you want. You get in life what you are.
—**Les Brown**

Most of the books written on sales should be gathered up, put in a big pile, and burned. When nothing is left except the ashes, we should throw a party. Why? Most of the sales literature is dysfunctional. The underlying metaphor is war—you against your prospective clients. The fundamental premise is to sell to pain. Essentially, these books appeal to the worst part of your nature (selfishness) to exploit the weakest part of your prospective client's nature (fear).

What if there's a better way? What if we can take the best part of our nature (generosity) and use it to enable the best part of our prospect's nature (vision)? What if we could be truly human as we sell to others, and in so doing enable them to be truly human?

Desire, not fear, is the primary emotion. While both are fundamental, fear only exists because at first there was a desire. People often lose track of their heartfelt desires because they become overwhelmed with worry. When you help someone achieve their noble, heartfelt desires, you are taking the best part of your nature and using it to help them express the best part of theirs. As you do this, you'll notice how "coincidentally" you keep showing up in people's lives at the right time.

We share many characteristics with other life forms on earth. One characteristic that is unique to humans, however, is our ability to dream. I don't mean the type of dreaming we do when we are asleep. I mean our ability to use our faculty of imagination to develop new ideas and envision our future. This faculty is at the heart of what it means to be human. Show me a person with no dreams and I'll show you someone with no life. To live is to dream! People who are fully alive are pulled into the future by their vision. They are filled with deep desire to realize their vision. Understanding this is the key to having a productive life and a lucrative career in sales.

You're reading this book because you want to improve your situation. This book will give you new insights. It will also give you new skills. Both will change your life. The insights in this book come from personal experience and years of study and application. If you manage a sales team, this book will show you the necessary conditions you must create for your team's success. If you've been selling for a long time, this book will give you fresh insights into why what you're doing is working and how to take your game to the next level. If you've never formally sold anything before, this book will give you practical steps and tools to accelerate your career.

How This Book is Organized

Human-to-Human Selling is organized into three parts.

In Part 1, we look at the practical changes needed to be successful today. We'll explore the H2H selling strategy in detail. We'll look at how to ask better and more strategic questions and how to tell better and more engaging stories. To be truly successful in sales today, it comes down to one simple goal: to understand and support the buying cycle. We must understand what people want and need and align with the natural, emotional pull that comes from people who want to improve their state. And we'll also explore how similar the buying cycle is to that other symbiotic phenomenon: marriage.

In Part 2, we explore the conceptual underpinning for a more human approach to sales. We will tale a brief look back in time for a historical perspective on the changes we are facing today. If we understand how people reacted to similar phenomena in the past, we can get insight into how people are likely to behave in the future. We'll distinguish a symbiotic partner from the more common term "the trusted advisor." The difference is less in the visible behaviors and more in the posture. A trusted advisor, no matter how much you trust him or her, is still fundamentally a supplier. But a symbiotic partner has skin in the customer's game. A symbiotic partner moves side-by-side with the customer—they work together as partners to provide value to each other and to the world. After we learn about the basic roles of buyer and seller in human-to-human (H2H) selling, we'll learn about the five stages of the customer relationship life cycle.

Finally, in Part 3, we'll explore the human-to-human enterprise, understanding better how the sales process fits into it—and how sales can lead the way in establishing a more client-focused corporate strategy. We'll learn about the enterprise life cycle and the coveted Winners' Quadrant, the ultimate prize for symbiotic business relationships.

Throughout the book I use the term prospective clients rather than prospects, as the term prospective clients connotes the moral obligation we have to look after those people who come to us for help. I use the term buyers to refer to decision-making executives (not people in the purchasing department) within client and prospective client organizations, and I use the terms offerings and products to refer to both products and services. I also alternate between speaking to the sales practitioner and the chief executive. If you are a sales professional, it's important for you to understand the perspective of those above you in the organization so you can more effectively communicate with them and get them to understand the context required for you to be successful. If you are a chief executive, it's important for you to see how sales professionals can behave differently to enable your firm to become more strategic to your customers. If you're a sales leader, it's vital for you to work from both perspectives.

Whether you're a sales professional, a chief executive, or a manager in between, this book is going to teach you how to incorporate symbiosis into your sales strategy so you can not only create those win-win solutions and profitable, long-term relationships, but maybe even be the catalyst to transform your entire company so that it's structured to serve rather than fight and exploit customers.

This book is going to teach you how to get more out of life by giving more. Anything that you want for your life, you can have. Many years ago the late Zig Ziglar said you can get anything you want in life if you help enough other people get what they want. He was right.

My Personal Story

My path to selling was an unconventional one. It began when I quit school at age seventeen. Of course, this caused some problems at home, and I was told to go back to school or leave home. I thought I knew everything. So I left.

Having nowhere to go, I found a cold concrete stairwell and lived in it. From there, I got entangled in a criminal element. I watched in awe as guns and copious amounts of drugs changed hands. Seeing this raw underworld "up close and personal" scared me, and I knew I didn't want this kind of life. So when I turned eighteen I got my taxi license and was able to rent a bachelor apartment. But I kept falling behind on my rent, and eventually I was threatened with eviction if I didn't come up with the rent money in forty-eight hours.

I had to really hustle for every one of those 48 hours in order to come up with the rent. I took caffeine pills to keep myself from sleeping. I don't recommend this! I learned later in life that people die from sleep deprivation! Anyway, I did what I had to do. I paid my rent. I went home and slept and woke up around twenty hours later. When I woke up, I felt exhausted. I realized something had to change in my life. I realized I needed an education in order to have more choices. I decided to go back to school. I finished high school and went on to university. In the process, I discovered sales. I loved it and realized it's what I really wanted to do. I devoted myself to it. I lived and breathed it.

Along the way I learned some keys to big success in sales. If you read this book carefully and apply the concepts, you'll dramatically improve your sales performance regardless of where you are today. I've helped novices get on the fast track and I've helped top producers earn even more. I can help you.

Business is so much more fulfilling when we commit to helping others achieve their dreams and aspirations. If we are only wrapped up in our own goals, we become insensitive to others. Let's commit to only doing business that is win-win-win (for our clients, their clients, and their employees). Let's settle for nothing less in our business relationships. In so doing, we will build economic engines that can't help but go from strength to strength. We'll also be more humane with each other, and we'll build a better world.

It's About Helping Others

Your value is in what you do for others.

I fell in love with sales because it's about helping people. There's no greater job in the world, in my opinion, because the salesperson gets to create win-win solutions and profitable, long-term partnerships between two parties who were made for each other—the company and the right-fit customer. It should be fulfilling, and it should be fun.

But what I've seen in my sales experience and sales training is that most salespeople—even if they started by falling in love with sales as I did—aren't having fun. Quite the contrary. They're plagued by worry and they feel burdened. They say things like, "When I reach [insert some personal goal here], then I'll have fun." The problem with that is you'll probably quit before you get there. Or lose yourself in the process.

I believe I know why sales isn't very fun or fulfilling for most people.

Some of the most popular sales training programs have taught us to make adversaries out of the very people we want to help and who our company was created to serve (and actually can't live without). Have you ever noticed how many sales experts use war as the underlying metaphor for selling? Not only is this discouraging, it's very difficult to broker a deal between two parties who don't trust each other.

Even worse, most salespeople are evaluated and rewarded not on how well they build profitable relationships with right-fit customers over time, but on short-term sales quotas—the same way some singles boast about "scoring" with the opposite sex, without realizing that the higher their "score" gets the less likely they are to find a truly satisfying (and ultimately fulfilling) long-term relationship.

The solution is a simple concept that shows us that differences don't have to divide but could in fact be the catalyst for a new relationship that is greater than the sum of its parts. It's the magic behind a marriage that really lasts until "death do us part." It's even embedded in your cellular structure. This concept is called *symbiosis*, and it's as natural as breathing. You breathe in oxygen and exhale carbon dioxide. Trees inhale carbon dioxide and exhale oxygen. Life is beautiful when it's symbiotic!

The key to understanding H2H selling is understanding symbiosis as a function of desire. Most sales training has taught us to focus on finding pain or fear. Desire is what matters. Desire is the fuel that drives innovation. It's the fuel that drives accomplishment. It is the link between the invisible and the visible. Desire takes what's in the mental dimension and manifests it in the physical dimension.

Here's how it works. Someone, let's call them a creator, gets an idea in their mind. They use their imagination to work with the idea. As the idea takes shape in the creator's mind, he/she becomes filled with desire. This desire acts like a powerful magnet. It draws the resources and the people (i.e., you) to them. With these resources, the creator can now act in new ways to drive the new results that will bring about the new reality.

Steve Jobs was a great example of this. He had a vision of a new breed of technology. He wanted to create technology that was beautiful, not just functional. This idea floated in his mind for some time before it really began to take shape. Once it took shape, he had an unstoppable desire to manifest his vision. As a result of that desire, Sir Jonathan Ive showed up with the talents he developed over time and became the lead designer of many of Apple's products including the MacBook Pro, iMac, MacBook Air, iPod, iPod Touch, iPad, and iPad Mini. With

Jonathan and the other resources that "showed up," Steve Jobs was able to manifest his vision and create a new reality. The new technologies that Steve brought into the world have become essential resources for others to manifest their dreams. For example, this book (my dream) was written on an iMac and MacBook Air!

This is the process:

1. A creator is inspired by an idea;
2. The idea triggers deep desire;
3. Desire attracts new resources;
4. New resources enable new actions;
5. New actions enable new results;
6. New results create a new reality;
7. The new reality becomes a new resource for another creator as the process is repeated.

The key to understanding H2H selling is understanding symbiosis as a function of desire. The new reality becomes the resource in somebody else's realization process. This process is repeated every day. Sir Jonathan Ive's talents were once a dream. Based on that dream, resources showed up in his life to help him manifest his dream. Once the dream is manifested and becomes reality, it is a resource for the manifestation of the dreams of others.

Speaking of Apple, have you noticed Apple doesn't sell to pain? Apple's brand is about aspiration. It's for those people who want to change the world. Steve Jobs said Apple's core value is "we believe that people with passion can change the world for the better."

This is the high road. Rather than sell to people's fears, sell to their desires. Desire is like a fax machine ringing. When fax machines were invented, we were surprised to see that a document with an image in one location could be perfectly replicated in another. When desire is activated, get ready. Something in the invisible realm is about to be replicated in the visible realm. As a sales professional, become a part of this process. Help creators create! Filling up the emotional tank with fear may get you one sale. Filling up the emotional tank with desire, inspiration, and confidence in a dream will build a lifelong friendship.

As you are helping your clients realize their vision, others are helping you realize yours. We all need each other. When you don't plug into this process, you're forced to be a commodity. Dream realization is the opposite of commoditization. When you help someone realize their dreams, you become a valued partner.

It's true that the balance of power between customer and company has changed. Whereas companies used to control product information and thus hold the power in the relationship, the Internet has released that power to the masses. Some companies believe that increased transparency and access to information will threaten profitability. But if you master the concept of H2H selling, increased transparency and your customers' increased access to information will actually increase your profitability, because you'll be able to connect to your right-fit customers more easily than ever. You'll be able to relate as human beings rather than adversaries and will most likely become friends in the process.

I believe that when we find the desire and the path in life that's unique to us, that connection with our true path and desire releases an energy that's unique to us, and we will have the time of our lives. That kind of enjoyment and energy is what will draw others to us and ultimately make us a better sales professional and better person. If sales is your symbiotic path, my desire is that the ideas in this book will give you the vision, the strategy, and the tools to connect you to that passion as they have for the many others who have been exposed to them.

PART ONE

HUMAN-TO-HUMAN SELLING:
GETTING ENGAGED

Chapter 1

FOLLOW THE BUYING CYCLE

Buying is a profound pleasure.
—**Simone de Beauvoir**

One of my earliest memories of sales is when I was recruited as a fourteen-year-old by Encyclopedia Britannica (the most authoritative source of knowledge in the 1970s) to sell their comprehensive set of encyclopedias to parents. I was given a script and then trained on how to handle various objections by category. Looking back, the whole process was presumptuous and manipulative. Encyclopedia Britannica assumed it knew what was best for parents and their children. Whatever concerns the parents raised about acquiring such a comprehensive set of encyclopedias, we really didn't take seriously. All we wanted was for them to buy our product.

Ironically, my mother was a single parent and couldn't afford Encyclopedia Britannica. She bought us a set of Funk & Wagnall's encyclopedias from the local grocery store and we loved them. We consulted them often, and for our age they were excellent. Later in high school, I would go to the library to access the Encyclopedia Britannica when I needed to do more heavy-duty research.

I was good at following the script and made some pretty good commissions for a fourteen-year-old. I can remember sitting in many living rooms and dining rooms, making my pitch and stick-handling the various objections as they arose. The whole process was a system. I learned to read my prospective clients and anticipate their objections. By following the process I was trained in, I was able to retrieve the appropriate response to each objection from my mental toolkit and manipulate my potential buyers into feeling guilty about not putting a high enough priority on their children's education.

The Product-Push Trap

The product-push trap is easy to fall into. We naturally see the world from our own perspective. If we can convince others to see the world from our perspective, they too will recognize the virtues of our offerings. It's a trap because it's the easy way. Encyclopedia Britannica could hire me and others like me at the tender age of fourteen and set us up for success by following their program. Their emphasis was on training us on their product, which they knew well. They also knew all the objections we might encounter, and they could train us on these objections. All we had to do was follow the process and then persuade, coax, and cajole buyers into buying our product.

Once the deal was closed, it wasn't our concern what they actually did with the product. I'm sure many parents regretted buying such a comprehensive set of encyclopedias for their children. Perhaps the children never touched them. We were never asked to follow up and inquire about the actual use of the product.

At heart, this product-push approach is rooted in our misunderstanding of value, and this misunderstanding of value is rooted in Industrial Age assumptions. In the Industrial Age, those who owned the means of production defined value. The producers were those who could afford to invest in land, buildings, and equipment. With these assets, they could pull resources from the ground, put them through a process, and convert them to finished products. This process added value to raw materials. Value belonged to the producers.

Old Approach: Value = raw materials + value-added process

The Foundation of Today's Popular Sales Processes

Fast-forward to the new millennium. A lot has changed since the 1970s, but our sales processes haven't changed much. I still come across many organizations that use a sales process not dissimilar to the one Encyclopedia Britannica used. In essence, they assume they know better than their potential clients what is right for them. They train their sales team on the features and benefits of their product or service, and they also train them on how to handle objections and close the deal.

I recently examined the origin of a very popular sales process developed in the 1970s. The founder of this process was sick and tired of buyers pushing him around. He developed this system to control buyers and ensure they did not take advantage of him. That system, though still popular today, is dysfunctional and is built on the assumption that, and I quote, "buyers are liars" and salespeople must protect themselves from buyers. It is rooted in suspicion and pits seller against buyer. Even with the best intentions, salespeople using methodologies like this cannot help but engage in a contest of wills with buyers, similar to boxers in the ring.

This type of selling, as dysfunctional as it was, worked for two reasons. First, buyers did not see themselves as having authority. Buyers in the 1970s were passive. Their psychology was completely different from the psychology of today's "Google anything you want to" buyer. Second, their environment was simple. It did not have the layers of technological, operational, and cultural complexity that today's buyer must navigate. Sellers could force their solutions on buyers without worrying about what it would take to actually implement the changes required to make the solution successful.

Most of the popular sales processes used today were developed in the 1970s or earlier. While this does not automatically mean they are obsolete, what is noteworthy is how much the world has changed in the last three to four decades. As far as sales and marketing go, the pivotal point is 1991, which marked the introduction of the World Wide Web. Prior to 1991, access to information was difficult. We depended on corporations to "educate" us. Post 1991, we have taken education into our own hands. The rise of Google is a reflection of the rise of buyer empowerment.

As buyers, we educate ourselves. Google gives us a blank page with a single text box. Information is served up to us when we need it and as we need it. This relationship with Google influences our relationship with potential suppliers. We want them to behave like Google. "Don't tell us what you think we need to know. Let us ask you for the information we need when we need it, and be as precise and concise as possible."

Information is power. Choice is power. Today, primarily as a result of the Internet and globalization, power has shifted from those with the means of production to those with the means for consumption. Consumers have a choice and they have access to vast amounts of information. Gone are the privileged positions sales practitioners used to enjoy as the sole fountain of information. Years ago, salespeople showed up with the product catalog and informed the buyer about what was new. Today, buyers simply Google whatever information they want to find. Regardless of what is being purchased, one can become reasonably well-informed within a matter of hours. One can access experts instantly and find out the key advantages and disadvantages of any solution, the major providers of any solution, and their track record. In today's market, not only is education a mouse click away, but so is your competition.

Why Have a Sales Team?

If consumers can educate themselves and assess their options online, why have salespeople at all? Why not just sell online? For many companies, this is in fact what they are doing. Buyers are reasonably well-educated, they know what they want, and once they find your site, if everything checks out, they'll order what they need. Salespeople appear to be an expensive luxury.

But salespeople are needed for the very same reason the old selling techniques no longer work: the buyer's world has become more complex. Because of this increasing complexity, simply "handling objections" and forcing the close is irresponsible. As I mentioned, when I was selling the Encyclopedia Britannica, we weren't trained to care about how our product was actually used. In this age when consumers have as loud a voice in the market as producers, producers are forced to care about how their solutions are adopted. Social media has forced producers to have a social conscience.

New Approach: Value = client perception of value/product cost

We must now concern ourselves with the actual improved condition our salespeople promise. Consequently, we must be more concerned than we have been traditionally about who we do business with. Selling to someone simply because they have a need, the authority to make decisions, and the budget is no longer good enough. We must discern that they are serious about the change they plan to implement and have the tenacity to stick with it until the transformation is achieved. Their well-being and our reputations are at stake!

Another way for salespeople to demonstrate their value in this new environment is to think and communicate in terms of outcomes rather than products. So rather than focus on what the product is, focus instead on what it does. As Peter Drucker said, "Clients don't buy products, they buy results," or, as most of us have heard, "Clients don't buy drills, they buy holes." We need to go deeper with this understanding as we're competing with people who also understand this. Let's realize that people actually want more than holes. Some want to get a job done. Others want the expert feeling that comes from owning professional-grade tools, such as a DeWalt or Hilti drill. In the end, a $40 Craftsman drill will drill the same hole as a $400 DeWalt or Hilti drill. A deeper understanding of the buyer will enable us to address the differences in needs. Some buyers want to be seen a certain way, and they want to feel a certain way. To some it's just a hole. To others it's part of their journey to self-actualization.

Understanding how and why buyers buy will result in engaging potential clients much earlier in their buying cycle as we will align with their heartfelt needs rather than try to force them to align with our products.

Clients are constantly looking for better ways to achieve the outcomes they want. If you, as the producer, continue to concentrate on the process of making widgets, or the mass marketing of those widgets, rather than on delivering high-value outcomes, your future success is at risk.

Remember, not only has the voice of the client been amplified, so has their power of choice. Chris Anderson's *The Long Tail* does a remarkable job of showing us how the manipulation of the masses to accept "hits" is becoming increasingly difficult. According to Anderson, if you were to graph a company's products along the x-axis from most popular to least against the number of purchases on the y-axis, you'd see a head followed by a tailing off (the long tail). The long tail represents the increasing demand for niche products and an opportunity for new profits as increasing digitization enables this demand to be met profitably. Clients are supporting those vendors who can give them exactly what they need, and even those vendors on the extreme far right of the long tail are finding ways to service their clients profitably.

Buyer-Pull Replaces Product-Push

Successful change and discerning the necessity for change are both based in an agitated emotional state. When buyers realize that the status quo is no longer sufficient, and that there is a better way, they become agitated. The gap between where they are and where they want to be becomes intolerable. It is this emotional agitation that I refer to as "buyer-pull." Buyer-pull is like a magnetic force. The buyer forms a vision of what's possible and becomes emotionally committed to that state. This emotional agitation compels the buyer to seek out the resources that will close the gap.

Today's sales practitioner must focus less on his or her product or service and much more on the buyer's emotional state. The buyer's emotional agitation is what invites change, and ultimately it's what drives implementation and makes the change stick. Like flying an airplane, where takeoff and landing are the most challenging parts of the flight, leaving the status quo and ultimately replacing it with a new status quo are the most difficult parts of the buying process and require a significant amount of emotional energy. Today's sales practitioner must possess the emotional intelligence to ensure sufficient emotional agitation exists to get through the buying process and, after the purchase, that sufficient emotional agitation exists to drive through the political upheaval and the change-management process required to establish a new status quo.

This means overhauling the sales process to be much more buyer-centric. Each step in your sales process should support the buying process, ultimately focusing on helping the buyer achieve their intended outcomes. When you focus on delivering real value at each stage of the buying process and on achieving the buyer's desired outcome, handling objections becomes obsolete. Handling objections is akin to forcing your will on your buyer. Instead of handling objections, your focus needs to be on both parties understanding the risks involved and developing an approach to mitigate the risks. Handling objections is adversarial. Understanding and mitigating risks is collaborative. Any sales process that is not collaborative will eventually backfire.

As we shift from the old Industrial Age-based way of selling to the modern buyer-focused selling, we need to develop new perspectives, skills, and approaches. Decades ago we pursued mass markets. We didn't think of individual customers. Today we understand the importance of looking after customers. Our sales thinking, however, is still based in a product-push philosophy. In order to develop a buyer-pull approach, we must understand individual buyers at the level of their decision making. This starts with understanding the mind and motivations of the buyer. We turn our attention there next.

The Mind of the Buyer

American physician and neuroscientist Paul MacLean formulated a model for how the human brain works and explains it at length in his book *The Triune Brain in Evolution* (Springer, 1990). In summary, MacLean shows that our human brain has three key structures:

1. **The reptilian complex.** This structure is formed first and is based in the stem of the brain. It governs much of our instinctual responses and is fundamentally concerned with our growth and survival. MacLean observes that the brains of lizards and other reptiles share a similar structure.

2. **The mammalian brain**. This complex governs our emotional life. MacLean also refers to this structure as the limbic system. A number of brain structures work together to comprise the limbic system, including but not limited to the amygdala, hippocampus, and hypothalamus. The role of the limbic system in decision-making is only now becoming fully appreciated.

In the past we relied on the casualties of war to gain deeper understanding of how the brain works. Neuroscientists would observe the damaged part of the brain and the associated loss in neurological functions. With the advent of modern imaging technology, neuroscientists can now study the functioning of the brain in real time as healthy subjects engage in various activities.

One of the most astonishing findings is the role of emotions in decision-making. Prior to this we believed humans were rational beings who felt emotion. Today, we realize humans are emotional beings that have the ability to think. Emotion comes first, and it's what powers the mind to think.

When something is important to us, the limbic system bathes the mind in emotion. This emotion activates and recruits the rational parts of our mind to pay attention and analyze the relevant data.

3. **The prefrontal cortex.** This structure located behind the forehead is responsible for our higher-level functioning. The cortex governs all the things we can do as humans that animals are unable to do. The ability

to work with abstract concepts, speak languages, and engage in reason is all done in the cortex. It is becoming more apparent, however, that rather than lead us to a decision, the cortex uses reason to help us justify decisions already arrived at by the limbic and reptilian systems.

Goals and the Nonrational Mind

A further insight neuroscience has brought us is that our emotions are rooted in goals. Said another way, it's because we have goals that we become emotional. Our emotional states act like a radar system. When we feel good, it's because our goals are on the way to being fulfilled. When we feel bad, our limbic system is trying to warn us that we are not going to achieve our goals and we need corrective action.

Our goals fall into one of two categories: 1) *approach goals* and 2) *avoidance goals*.

Approach goals are the things we want to accomplish. They are positive goals. We can form an image of them in our mind's eye. Avoidance goals are different. They are stated in the negative. They are the things we feel threatened by that we want to avoid.

Why is this distinction important?

Avoidance goals trigger fear.

Approach goals trigger desire.

Fear and desire are our two foundational emotions. All other emotions are derivatives of these two emotions. We are either energized to move toward someone or something or we are energized to move away. Energy comes from our emotions not our reason.

This insight negates what sales trainers have been teaching for years. Historically sales trainers have taught sales professionals to look for and sell to needs.

Don't Sell to Needs—Sell to Priorities

If you want to outperform your competition, stop selling to needs. Traditional sales training takes it for granted that if you uncover what someone needs, you can sell your solution to them. This is no longer true.

Every business has more needs than it can address. Consequently, businesses learn to live with pain. What you see as a true need, your prospective decision-maker most likely sees as a tolerable inconvenience. Every year organizations budget their expenses for the coming year. Part of this process includes items and part of it excludes items. It's not that the excluded items are unnecessary. It's that they are not a priority.

Prioritization is an emotional exercise. One thing means more to us than another based on our emotional disposition toward it. Emotions are rooted in goals. We have emotions because we have goals. As I said earlier, emotions inform us regarding the likelihood of something moving us closer to our goal or away from it. Positive emotions encourage us to go forward. Negative emotions force us to seek another course.

Needs and goals are not the same. Needs are the soil out of which goals emerge, but goals take precedence. For example, I might be thirsty and need a drink. However, I may have set a goal not to eat or drink for a period of time for health reasons. I will suppress my need in order to achieve my goal. Sacrificing the fulfillment of needs is often the price a buyer has to pay to achieve something more meaningful to them. Humans are creative by nature. Our imagination is a creative force. Once we develop a clear image of what we want and deep desire is triggered as a result, we will sacrifice the fulfillment of many needs to achieve our heartfelt desires.

How well do you understand what your existing and potential customers are trying to accomplish? What are they trying to achieve? How do you help? Don't assume that because you understand their needs, you understand their goals. Find out. Help them achieve their goals and notice how emotionally energized they become about working with you.

The Buying Process

The foundation of our sales process should be the buying process. We should no longer focus on selling; we must now focus on helping people buy. Helping them buy is about helping them pull the resources they need to accomplish the image they have in their mind. Everything a sales professional does should be in the best interests of the buyer. Sales professionals need to empathize with buyers in a way that we never have before. While sales is never a linear process, it helps to think about the steps in a linear/best-case scenario. Once we understand the principles of the sales process, we can adapt them dynamically in real time.

However, the steps of the sales process must be subordinate to the steps in the buying process. We must therefore understand the buying process before we unpack the steps in the selling process. One of the early pioneers in understanding the buying process is the author of *SPIN Selling*, Neil Rackham.

At thirty thousand feet, all buyers go through the same basic steps. Within your industry, there will be nuances and specific details, but at thirty thousand feet, the buying process is:

THE BUYING CYCLE

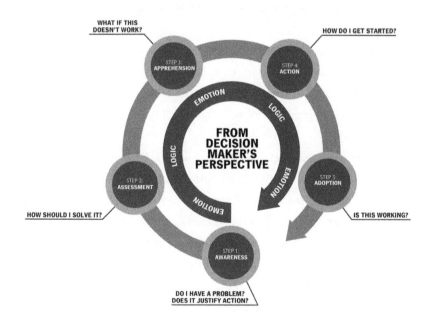

Figure 3.1. The Buying Process from the Decision Maker's Perspective

0. Status Quo. All buyers start with a status quo, which they regard as acceptable or even desirable. In many cases they are completely unaware of it. Something has to happen for the buyer to question their satisfaction with the status quo before a buying process can begin.

1. Awareness. The buyer begins to imagine a new future and becomes dissatisfied with the current state. Once the buyer becomes dissatisfied with the status quo, the potential to implement change emerges. When buyers see that the status quo no longer serves their purpose, they become open to considering alternatives. The emotional agitation the buyer experiences comes from two places: 1) frustration, when they become annoyed at the way things are being done and become increasingly concerned; and 2) desire, when they begin to imagine a better way and experience an increasing desire for things to improve. Note that the awareness is not an awareness of your product or service. It is an awareness of the insufficiency of their current situation. It is an awareness of the gap between where they are and where they could be.

2. Assessment. Once buyers realize they need to do something other than the status quo, they begin to explore options.

On one hand, neurological studies teach us that the mind hates gaps, and on impulse buyers will want to fill the gap with the first solution they see.

However, there's a part of us that also hates acting on impulse. There's a part of us that was socialized to control our impulses and detests the idea of jumping on the first solution we see. It needs to ensure we have explored all our options. This is especially true when multiple decision makers are involved. The assessment process involves getting clear about the outcome desired, establishing the criteria for making a decision, and evaluating alternatives against these criteria. This stage is governed by the rational mind.

3. Apprehension. Once the "best" alternative is selected, buyers immediately begin to consider the risks associated with the chosen alternative. They imagine all the things that could go wrong. At

this stage the status quo starts to appear attractive again. Buyers need to reassure themselves that they are in fact making the right decision, and should the risks begin to unfold, they have a sound strategy to deal with these risks. This stage is governed by a state of anxiety.

4. Action. At this stage buyers are ready to negotiate the agreement and sign off on the order form. They want clarity on what needs to be done to get the ball rolling. This stage is governed by reason. The buyer needs to understand how to initiate the process.

5. Adoption. The buyer now brings the solution into their environment. There are many eventualities that occur that the buyer couldn't predict. Changing the status quo is not so easy. It requires a significant amount of commitment from both the buyer and the seller to navigate the change process and enable the new solution to become established as the new status quo. When this happens, the buyer experiences fulfillment. If it doesn't happen, the buyer experiences resentment.

The remaining chapters in this section will explore each of these phases of the buying process in more detail, as well as what sales behaviors are appropriate at each stage. As you'll see, the buying process is very similar to the process of developing any kind of committed, long-term relationship, particularly of that leading up to another significant symbiotic relationship: marriage.

CEO Action Plan

- ❏ Get clear on your higher purpose (personally and professionally) and ensure your employees are engaged in that higher purpose.
- ❏ Get your intention right. It should not be to sell more. Ensure your sales team and everyone else in your company is committed to helping your buyers achieve more of their desired outcomes. Get them to see sales transactions as a natural outcome to helping buyers.
- ❏ Map out the typical buying process for your clients and figure out how your sales process adds value to it.

Sales Professional Action Plan

- ❏ Identify the emotional journey your buyers go through and understand clearly how you can help them through their journey.
- ❏ Look at your current sales funnel and identify where your buyers are in their buying cycle. Get clarity on what you could do next to help them move forward to the right solution.
- ❏ Stop handling objections. Understand the buyer's risks and collaborate with them in mitigating identified risks.
- ❏ Get clear on your higher purpose. Ensure your work is in line with what you want to become as a human being.

Chapter 2

PHASE ONE: AWARENESS

To become different from what we are,
we must have some awareness of what we are.
Eric Hoffer

As I've described the phases of the buying cycle to a variety of audiences, the metaphor that has always resonated is that of marriage. I suppose this should be a logical connection: for both the right-fit business relationship and a marriage, the goal is a deepening relationship of trust and partnership over time, albeit in different contexts. I met my wife at a reception. Hundreds of people were present and I noticed her right away. I went over and introduced myself. I was a complete stranger, but I was friendly and (hopefully) charming. We chatted briefly and then I asked her if she would join me for lunch. We had a great lunch. Now I was a desired supplier!

At the time, my wife was living in the UK. She was only here on vacation. She appreciated the fact that I asked her out to lunch. No one else had. It pays to be bold! She thought I was charming, engaging, and generous. She said she realized I was quite popular and she figured it was nice to meet me, but she wouldn't hear from me again. She was wrong. I wrote her every day (this was before email). She was touched by my commitment to her, and we became very close even though we were thousands of miles apart. She saw that I had a real interest. We became each other's trusted advisors.

The underlying emotions we both felt were supported by logic. We were married in a short space of time, but not without both of us logically evaluating the relationship. In just over a year we were married. Twenty-two years later, we continue to make each other happy and build our life together. We have a great life and two beautiful children. We went from complete strangers to soulmates. My "proposal" was one question. Think about it. The biggest contract in my life was based on a one-question proposal.

Think of how unproductive the typical sales approach would have been. It would have felt like I was in a military campaign. I would seek to outsmart her so I could conquer her. I would sell on fear. Instead of sharing our dreams, I would threaten her with being a spinster if she didn't marry me. I would propose prematurely, and if she objected I would be armed with objection-handling responses. I would not give up until my will prevailed. How dysfunctional! Do you "hunt" your friends? Why do you "hunt" your customers?

Personal relationships that grow from two strangers meeting to two engaged individuals formally "tying the knot" should develop naturally as both parties become increasingly engaged. These two symbiotic relationships develop in very much the same pattern, which should reassure us that human-to-human selling really is just about being human. My hope is that presenting the buying cycle in this way will free you to follow your relational instincts when developing your sales strategy.

In the beginning, for those who decide they will eventually move toward a marriage relationship, the status quo is being happily single. Then something happens—whether it's a close friend getting married, hitting a certain age, or a sense of the biological clock ticking—that creates an awareness that one's single status is no longer quite as desirable as it once was. In response, the person begins exploring their options. They may find themselves going out to places where they are most likely to meet their ideal mate, for example, rather than just going out to have a good time.

A similar thing happens in the Awareness stage of the buying cycle. The buying process begins when the buyer becomes aware that the status quo is no longer desirable. Here's what happens in the Awareness stage:

Buyer State of Mind: The buyer is becoming increasingly aware that something is wrong with the status quo. He/she is becoming emotionally agitated. The fundamental emotions in this stage are frustration and desire: frustration that things that should be happening are not happening, or things that shouldn't be happening are, and the desire for a better future.

Buyer Objectives: During this stage of the buying process, the buyer goes from being satisfied and happy with the status quo to becoming concerned that the status quo may interfere with his/her ability to achieve his/her goals. The objectives in this stage are 1) to understand the inadequacies of the status quo, 2) to confirm that these inadequacies really do present a challenge to the achievement of their goals, and 3) to determine if there is a reasonable alternative to the status quo.

Salesperson's Objectives: The salesperson's objectives should be 1) to get the buyer's attention, 2) to secure a meeting with the buyer, 3) to jointly explore the inadequacies of the status quo with the buyer, 4) to help the buyer understand the nuances and broader implications of their challenges, 5) to discern if sufficient emotional agitation exists to complete the buying cycle and implement change, and 6) to get approval to do further investigation throughout the firm to uncover the real issues.

Risk: The seller engages the buyer in exploring solutions before confirming that there is sufficient emotional agitation to complete the buyer's journey and actually act on and implement the solution, resulting in opportunities that eventually stall in the sales funnel.

Getting Buyer Attention

Historically, there has been a divide between sales and marketing. Very few companies have their sales and marketing teams working together seamlessly. The current economy, however, is forcing the issue. With more demanding buyers, more niche-oriented competitors, and longer sales cycles, salespeople are being forced to think like marketers and marketers are being forced to think like salespeople.

Both sales and marketing have their own funnels. Marketing must now directly tie the end of their funnel to the beginning of the sales funnel. Moreover, the output of the sales funnel must tie back into the marketing funnel. Every dollar spent on marketing must be measurable and show clear return on investment. Every lead generated for the sales force must be accounted for.

Traditional marketing focuses on creating *brand awareness*. This is not the same as the buying cycle stage of Awareness (i.e., *buyer awareness*). Brand awareness is focused on positioning and pushing solutions. Buyer awareness is focused on identifying and understanding problems. Brand awareness assumes buyers are looking for solutions; however, this is not where the buying journey begins. The buying journey begins with buyers facing undesirable symptoms. They are trying to understand why they are facing these conditions and what they can do to address them. In a "pull" world, buyers begin their journey searching for understanding first and solutions second. Those buyers in search of understanding tend to be senior executives. When the problem is finally understood, it is delegated to lower-level resources to find and implement solutions.

If your marketing is focused solely on positioning solutions, you exclude yourself from engaging with senior executives earlier in the buying cycle. Moreover, you are being invited to engage with potential buyers along with your competitors. It's a double-whammy. You end up working with junior resources who are looking for a commodity and want you to explain to them why your price is so high.

Another problem with brand-awareness marketing is that it is extremely expensive and almost impossible to measure. Companies with huge budgets tend to win this game. They succeed in creating mindshare for the sales team, but they do so by spending unnecessarily large amounts of money. Moreover, they never know which specific initiatives led to their success. Today, CEOs and CFOs expect more from marketing, and they are questioning every dollar spent. Marketing executives must get ahead of this scrutiny.

Measure Everything

Marketers must carefully plan their campaigns and set up clear measurement criteria to determine which campaigns are successful and how to increase their effectiveness over time. These metrics include but are not limited to: total reach, number of inquiries, number of first meetings, number of proposals, number of sales, meetings-to-reach ratio, closing ratio, conversion rate, acquisition cost, cost per contact, cost per meeting, profit results, and ROI. Marketers must clearly track all activity through the marketing funnel to the sales funnel. The marketing funnel should be comprised of three key stages:

1. **Reach:** the number of people in the suspect base that will be touched by a specific campaign
2. **Enquiry:** the number of people who respond positively to a campaign by initiating a conversation
3. **First meetings:** the number of people who are sufficiently interested such that they are willing to meet with a salesperson to learn how the firm might address their specific challenges (i.e., qualified leads)

The concept of reach may be an old one, but it's still an important metric in effective sales and in human-to-human selling. All marketing today must be oriented toward creating buyer awareness and generating qualified leads for the sales team. Every campaign must be measured in terms of the number of first meetings it generates for the sales team. And every sales professional must be scrutinized in terms of his or her ability to convert first meetings into sales.

Linking Funnels

The end of the marketing funnel is the beginning of the sales funnel. First meetings should represent the top of the sales funnel. All activities prior to the first meeting represent part of the marketing funnel even if salespeople are engaged in them. Yes, sales and marketing must learn to work together. So much so that in some organizations the sales and marketing funnels are starting to overlap. Inbound marketers are participating in sales functions, and enlightened sales professionals are embracing marketing approaches.

All opportunities must be tied to a specific campaign in order to connect all sales activity to the marketing activity. Once a first meeting is successfully concluded, the sales funnel should be comprised of three key phases:

1. **Diagnose:** The buyer is willing to work with the sales professional to help him or her understand the situation and develop a solution.
2. **Propose:** The buyer is clear about the challenge they are facing and what your firm can do about it, and they are open to receiving clear documentation on the specific way you can work with them to resolve their challenges.
3. **Close:** The buyer, ready to take action to resolve their challenges, is now negotiating with you and completing necessary paperwork to initiate a project.

The energy to move through the sales funnel should come from the buyer not the seller. It is the buyer who is trying to achieve something. The seller is there to help. The buyer moves through the sales funnel willingly because they see it as a means to an end. You know the buyer is willingly moving through the funnel when he or she commits more time to meet with you. The moment you have difficulty getting the buyer's time, it means they have difficulty seeing how you can get them where they are going. Buyers that are not ready to buy should be taken out of the sales funnel and put back into an automated marketing funnel through a drip or nurturing campaign.

Phases versus Steps

Many organizations we consult with tell me they have more than three steps in their sales process. I don't disagree. Your sales process, however, is not the same as your sales funnel. Managing the sales funnel is about managing the phases that opportunities go through as they mature. The steps you go through to make a sale are not the same as the phases that a sales opportunity will go through. By way of analogy, what you do to harvest fruit is separate from the phases that fruit goes through as it matures. Fruit is initially unripe, then it's ripe, and then it's consumed— or it spoils if it's not eaten. The steps to harvest fruit might involve planting, tilling, spraying, inspecting, picking, etc. The steps you go through to harvest might be very different from the steps I go through, but the phases the fruit will go through are universal. The same is true with funnel management. Phases must not be confused with activities.

Wash, Rinse, Repeat

The end of the sales funnel is the beginning of the marketing funnel. In other words, existing clients must not be neglected. Marketing must now engage in a separate set of campaigns that reach the entire client base, generate enquiries from existing clients, and lead to first meetings with the sales team to discuss new challenges/opportunities. To make the most of your sales and marketing investment, accurate metrics must be gathered for each phase of the marketing and sales funnel. Getting a handle on these metrics and putting them into a management dashboard is the key to ensuring every dollar invested in sales and marketing will provide increasing returns to the business. These metrics can be captured seamlessly if your CRM and accounting systems are set up properly and your sales and marketing teams learn to work together. Once these metrics are tracked and managed, sales and marketing will have tied the knot, and you will have a consistent cash-flow machine regardless of economic conditions.

One of the biggest setbacks I see to building a solid business is a lack of sufficient lead generation. When lead blackouts or dips occur, sales management becomes desperate. This often results in a sudden and heavy reliance on cold calling.

Let's face it: cold calling is for dinosaurs! In the past, salespeople were a source of information that was not easily discoverable. Google has changed that. Buyers don't want to be interrupted to learn about your product or service. When they have a need, they'll turn to the Internet and consume the information they need on a just-in-time basis. Your desperation for a sale doesn't magically create a space in your prospective client's busy day for her to accommodate you.

The ineffectiveness of cold calling drives the cost of client acquisition through the roof. Inbound marketing is proving to be a far more cost-effective and valuable way of generating leads. Not only does it reduce the expense of the sales force, it also provides greater value to the buyer looking for helpful information.

As the firm's sales team battles with cold calling, the prospective clients they are pursuing can sense the urgency and desperation. If you are a chief executive and you want your people to be at their best when calling on prospective clients, it is critical that you eliminate fear and desperation. The way to do this is with a proactive lead-generation system.

An effective system has three steps:

1. Launch campaigns that get attention and generate leads
2. Sell the leads on a first meeting—either by phone or in person
3. Triage the leads—diagnose, drip, drop, or delay

1. Launch campaigns that get attention and generate leads

Far too many companies invest in lead-generation strategies prior to considering what their ideal client looks like. As a result, they attract lots of attention from the wrong prospective clients. Once the ideal client is defined, it is much easier to determine how and where to find similar clients (we call these right-fit clients, as they may not be ideal but they are close). The next step, after profiling your ideal client, is to get the attention of right-fit clients and generate interest.

Your campaigns need to focus on giving value. In the Industrial Age, firms focused on cold calling. Cold calling is a system that was designed to serve vendors, not buyers. It is based on the belief that the vendor has every right to interrupt a buyer to tell him or her about the features and benefits of its products or services. Today, we can no longer assume that we have the right to barge in on buyers. We also have to be very careful about the emotional experience of buyers. Starting the relationship by annoying the buyer is not a great idea.

While designing your campaigns, spend time thinking about what value you can give away. Do you have intellectual property that you can convert into an interesting white paper? Do you have an instructional video that you can package digitally? What about a reprint article? Remember, even though you are not charging for this value, your potential client still has to pay attention and spend time consuming it. It really isn't free. For you, having these giveaways creates tremendous goodwill. Equally important, it enables you to measure the effectiveness of your campaigns. With these items in place, each campaign can be measured to evaluate how many people requested the value you have to offer.

2. Invite interested leads to a first meeting

Once you've earned their attention, your objective should be to get to know them better by scheduling first meetings. Think of a first meeting as a first date. When you ask someone out for a date, you take care of everything and you pay. Similarly, when you ask a prospective client for a first meeting, it is important that you make the initial investment. During this meeting, you need to demonstrate to your prospective clent that you provide relevant value. At the end of the first date, you have a decision to make: do you ask for a second date or not? If not, what do you do? Once you've gotten attention, it's important that you sell the right-fit client on giving you more of their time. Time, like money, is a currency that buyers trade for value. Granting you a first meeting is the buyer's way of communicating their expectation of receiving value by spending the currency of time with you. You need to structure this meeting so that the buyer is at ease, shares critical information with you, and enables you to determine your fit for the buyer. Based on this determination, you diagnose, drip, drop, or delay the opportunity.

3. Triage the leads

Based on the first meeting, the sales professional has a simple decision to make. Is this lead worth further investment?

Diagnose. If it is, the sales professional should end the first meeting by asking for a second meeting. Ideally, the first meeting is with a senior executive and the second meeting is scheduled for after the sales professional has met with his/her direct reports. Getting the executive to grant permission to the sales professional to perform this deeper diagnosis is a key objective of the first meeting. During the meetings with the direct reports, the objective is to properly diagnose and effectively develop the need. If the buyer is not ready or not a good fit, the lead should be dropped, dripped, or delayed.

Drop. This is self-explanatory. The lead is not a good fit and should not be pursued. Don't be afraid to drop leads. Saying no to many is the best way to do a great job for the ones you say yes to.

Drip. The lead is a good fit, but they are not ready to engage in a buying cycle today. They should be set on a schedule with predetermined periodic, educational communications to keep your firm top-of-mind until they are ready to engage in a buying decision. Each communication piece should provide significant value.

Delay. The lead is a good fit, but something needs to happen with them before they can seriously engage you. They have asked you to follow up with them in the near future but would not welcome periodic communications between now and then.

This process is what will drive growth in any economy. The simple step of using lead generation to drive first meetings and using first meetings to triage leads will ensure your sales team's funnel is always full with high-quality opportunities.

First Meetings

The single biggest predictor of a salesperson's success is their ability to secure first meetings with qualified buyers. This is such a significant event that I recommend calling it out as a distinct step in your sales process. It represents the link between the marketing funnel and the sales funnel. As such, it sits on top of the sales funnel and feeds the funnel. First meetings are with new prospective clients and existing clients. They are defined as a scheduled meeting (either face-to-face or by phone) with a qualified buyer regarding a new potential sales opportunity. The meeting should have a date, a time, and an agenda that have all been agreed to by the buyer. It is important that a disciplined process is followed during these meetings to ensure that both the buyer's and the seller's objectives are met for the Awareness phase. Incidentally, having an agenda is the best way to ensure your meeting stays on track to meet both the buyer's and the seller's objectives.

The Role of Emotion

The mistake most sales professionals make when meeting with executives is to focus on "finding the pain." This is a carryover from Industrial Age selling, and if one is not careful it can be a dysfunctional way of selling. Fundamentally, people are driven by one of two emotions: either desire or fear (accompanied by the actions of approach or evade). All of our other emotions are rooted in one of these two fundamental emotions. Feelings of triumph, cheerfulness, amusement, elation, delight, and joy all spring from desire. Conversely, feelings of disgust, anger, depression, sadness, envy, and irritation spring from fear. These two fundamental emotions represent the fuel of buying. Without sufficient fuel, potential purchases are stalled.

When selling to senior executives, it's important to establish a basis for a long-term relationship. Pain-based selling is short-term. Once the pain is relieved, the need for the relationship is also relieved. Moreover, all of us have the ability to tolerate pain. The longer we live with pain, the more we can tolerate it. Consequently, if you cannot make a quick sale with pain-based selling, it's likely that your deal will stall as the buyer learns to tolerate their situation. With pain-based selling, you'll likely make no sale, but even if you make a sale it will be difficult to maintain a long-term relationship.

Strategic objectives are longer-term. If you align with the need an executive has to achieve strategic objectives, your relationship will be longer-term as it takes time to achieve these goals. This is the heart of human-to-human selling. Humans are creative beings. We are at our best when we are creating. Rather than focusing on what people worry about, get engaged in their higher purpose. What is the invisible image they seek to bring into the visible realm? Once you understand the vision that drives them, and you can help them realize that vision, you'll become invaluable. Their desire for the expression of the vision will pull you into their world.

Another way to look at strategy is to see it as the collective desire of the organization. That is, everyone in the organization is there to help in the achievement of the strategy. If they are not aligned with the strategy, they shouldn't be there. The corporate strategy springs from the emotional desire of the key leader(s). Everyone must be aligned with this emotional desire.

Connecting with this underlying emotional energy is critical to long-term success.

Approach or Avoidance?

A lot of people think decision-making is a very logical exercise when in fact it is not. It is a very emotional exercise. Any logic that is engaged during the decision-making process is engaged because of emotion. As I stated before, there are only two categories of emotions—positive emotions rooted in desire and negative emotions rooted in fear. We know from neuroscience that emotions are tied to goals. Specifically, we have emotions *because* we have goals. And corresponding to our two primary emotions, we also have two primary types of goals: toward goals or away goals. We refer to goals we are moving toward as *approach goals* and goals we are moving away from as *avoidance goals*.

To the extent that the resources and people that show up in our lives help us move closer to our approach goals, they will trigger positive emotions. Resources and people that frustrate our ability to achieve our approach goals will trigger negative emotions. Likewise, the resources and people that show up in our lives and help us move away from our avoidance goals will trigger positive emotions, and the resources and people that show up in our lives that move us toward our avoidance goals will trigger negative emotions.

Unfortunately, most adults are governed by avoidance goals. They show up to work every day and stay until the end of the day to avoid getting fired—not because they sat down and planned their lives; not because they have a crystal clear vision of what they want and clearly understand how their workday maps into that vision. That's not the way human beings were designed. If you think about newborn babies, they initially start life with approach goals. For example, they want to be fed. They form a vision of being fed and they move toward that vision. A few months later, they notice everyone around them walking upright. They form a vision of themselves doing the same and marshal all their resources to achieve this approach goal.

As babies mature into children and then adults, bad things happen and they learn to worry. Through worry, they visualize all the bad things that could happen to them. These visual images become more pronounced and occupy more of their attention than the positive things they want. Most adults lose their personal vision and become dominated by avoidance goals. If you stop ten people on the street and ask them to crisply articulate for you what their lives will look like in five years, you will hear anything but crisp answers.

Typically, this is not the case with chief executives and business owners. They are the exception. When one leads an organization, one needs to lead with vision. One needs to spend time thinking about what the organization will look like in the future. One needs to consider the organization's strengths and weaknesses, and the opportunities and threats in the marketplace. The leader needs to craft a strategy that excites and inspires others. No leader would be successful standing up in front of thousands, hundreds, or even dozens of employees and declaring, "If we sacrifice and give this all we've got, maybe we will still be around in five years!" That would only inspire their people to polish up their resumes! We've helped many business leaders work through the hard task of thinking about their future and crafting both a personal and an organizational vision. This vision is an approach goal.

Avoidance goals should be subservient to approach goals. Approach goals should dominate our thinking, and avoidance goals should be formulated to keep us on track toward achieving our approach goals.

When we sell to chief executives and business owners, we need to connect with their approach goals. Everyone has avoidance goals, even the person at the top. However, when we connect to avoidance goals, we have to realize that these goals are fleeting. They are immediate. Present tense. Here and now. Once they are satisfied, they are gone.

Grudge Purchase

Avoidance goals also drive what I call a "grudge purchase." A grudge purchase is a purchase that you don't want to make, but you have to in order to escape negative consequences. Avoidance goals are not specific. They do not help us define what we want, just what we need to escape.

Think of insurance. If you're like most people, you don't wake up excited about buying insurance. You think about things you'd rather avoid and you realize you should have insurance to avoid these things. Because it's a grudge purchase, you try to put it off for as long as you can, and you try to buy as little as you can. If, like a typical insurance salesperson, you only sell to pain, you set yourself up for a grudge purchase. Your prospective client will want to wait as long as possible and will want to spend as little as possible. If someone else comes along offering something similar for less money, you'll be out of the picture.

The other problem with avoidance goals is they don't work well with the way our mind is designed to function. Think again of the newborn baby. It starts out with approach goals. Avoidance goals come later as the child begins to learn the concept behind the words *no* and *not*. Negation is a big concept. It generally isn't fully grasped until age two (the terrible twos!). Prior to age two and prior to language, the human mind doesn't work with negation. Negation requires rudimentary language. Prior to the development of rudimentary language, the human mind works with and manipulates images of what it wants. At this primary and most basic level, our imagination can't grasp negation.

Here's an example of what I mean. Right now, under no circumstances do I want you to think of an elephant. While you're not thinking about this elephant, don't think of it being completely pink—from trunk to tail. And certainly don't think of this pink elephant standing up on its hind legs, coming back down, and then spraying pink lemonade from its trunk. The reason I don't want you to imagine a pink elephant standing up on its hind legs and then coming back down and spraying pink lemonade out of its trunk is that it is a completely useless thing to do. Now, how successful were you in *not* forming this picture?

This is the way avoidance goals and worry work. When we worry about something, we form an image of the thing we don't want in our lives. The more attention we give to this image, the more it dominates our imagination. The more it dominates our imagination, the more we notice things that show up in our lives that are connected to it. As these things show up, they cause us to worry more. It sets up a vicious cycle. Eventually we act to escape; however, if we don't replace the image of what worries us with an image of what we actually want, we can end up sabotaging ourselves by being drawn to the things connected to our avoidance goals as the mind gravitates to what it sees in its imagination.

Yearning Purchase

The opposite of a grudge purchase is a "yearning purchase." A yearning purchase is a purchase that you really want to make. You daydream about taking possession of the object. Think of the many people who stood in line for hours to get a brand new iPhone. Anything can become a yearning. The yearning isn't really for the thing being sold. It's for the intangible benefit the thing enables (e.g., an enhanced self-image vs. a new iPhone). People will yearn for what you are selling if they can see what it will do for them. When you can show them how you can move them closer to their approach goals, they will yearn for what you are offering.

We experience pain and yearning differently. Initially, pain is intense and uncomfortable. We have an instinctive response to do whatever we can to escape the pain. Over time, however, pain loses its power. We have a built-in mechanism to tolerate pain. The longer we live with pain, the more we can live with it. Our experience with yearning is different. Yearnings gather power over time. The longer we live with a yearning for something, the more intolerable it becomes to live without it.

While we learn to live with pain, very few of us learn to live with intense desire. Desire, when it is not controlled, increases in intensity. Consequently, as long as you are selling something of real value, why settle for the risk of a grudge purchase when your team can enjoy the fascinating loyalty that comes from a yearning purchase?

Strategic Desire

As mentioned earlier, everyone who works for an organization must help the organization move toward its strategic objectives or they have no business being there. There is deep emotional energy behind strategic objectives. This energy is future-oriented. Tap into it and you will have long-term loyalty and will be able to align multiple people and departments behind your initiatives.

(I've developed a simple conversational methodology to uncover the strategic objectives of business executives and to combine the emotional energy of yearning with the emotional energy of avoidance. I call it A-SALE, and I'll walk you through it in the next chapter.)

Managing Face-to-Face Meetings

Hundreds of millions of dollars of goods and services will be purchased over the Internet this year. The Internet is a grand vending machine. Whatever people want is only a mouse click away. Yet businesses continue to employ salespeople to sell their services. Why?

Some things can't be sold through a vending machine. They require human interaction to provide explanation and to develop trust. Websites continue to evolve and provide increasingly helpful information. Every time your sales team shows up for a meeting, your prospective clients are wondering if they need to spend their time in this way. You need to ensure that every meeting your team has provides substantial value to your buyers—beginning with the very first meeting.

Remember, the key to your company's success is in the number of first meetings it has with qualified decision makers. But before that first meeting, all sales begin with a conversation. Within that initial conversation, if it goes well, trust is built. That conversation should lead to a first meeting. That first meeting, if it goes well, should lead to subsequent meetings. Each meeting either enhances trust or diminishes it.

One of the quickest ways for your team to unintentionally destroy trust is to show up for meetings unprepared. Senior executives have a lot on their plates. As you know, losing an hour or two in an unproductive meeting is frustrating at best. On the other hand, participating in a meeting that is well-orchestrated and leads to meaningful action is very fulfilling and one of the most effective ways to build trust with executives.

Whenever two or more people get together to try to accomplish something, by nature there will be competing agendas. Everyone is concerned with his or her own personal objectives, and anyone can be easily distracted. This is the underlying force that will compromise a sales professional's effectiveness in a first meeting. An effective salesperson will keep everyone on the same page and combine competing agendas into one mutually beneficial agenda.

The only way this can be done is through three clear steps: 1) careful preparation, 2) flawless execution, and 3) effective follow-up.

1. Careful Preparation

In all the years I have been selling and coaching others to sell, I have seen less than 5 percent of sales professionals who prepare effectively for sales meetings. Salespeople typically have lots of product knowledge, a quick mind, and a gift for speaking. Armed with these talents, they feel invincible. They make a quick assessment of what the client needs, review their pitch, and show up for the meeting.

Buyers are no better. Very few buyers demand an agenda beforehand. Most will simply schedule the time in their calendars. The salesperson will show up at the appointed time and both seller and buyer will navigate the meeting in real time. Often, people who were supposed to be in the meeting won't show up (something came up), people who weren't invited will show up (someone thought it would be a good idea to invite them), and the sequence the seller was expecting is quickly jettisoned.

The challenge is this: preparing for a meeting is hard work for sales professionals because they have to think through what they need to accomplish. If they are not in the habit of thinking in this way and they have a growing to-do list nagging at them in the background, it is much easier to skip preparation and "wing it."

The unrealized danger of "winging it" is that many sales professionals are relatively successful even when they wing it because of their quick minds. What goes unrealized, however, is how much more successful they could have been and how much they could have shortened their sales cycle had they engaged in careful preparation.

To prepare for a sales meeting, sales professionals need to do the following. First, they need to review whatever information they currently have about the buyer. Second, they need to be clear in their own mind about what additional information they need to uncover and what they want the buyer to do as a result of meeting with them.

Review whatever information you currently have about the buyer.
For those opportunities that merit greater attention, you'll need to do your homework. When you do get in front of your buyer, you want them to detect that you are a professional and that you know their business. This will go a long way to establishing credibility and trust. Start with the buyer's industry. How well do you know it? Every industry has a history. What are the significant events that have taken place in your prospective client's industry? Years ago when I was a sales practitioner, I focused

on the telecommunications industry. The deregulation of this industry was a defining moment. Anyone selling into the telecommunications industry and not understanding when and how deregulation impacted the industry would not come across as credible. You would also need to understand industry jargon. The telecommunications industry is peppered with three-letter initialisms (e.g., TLAs). If you sell to this industry and don't know the jargon, you are immediately perceived as an outsider. Every industry has jargon. If you learn the jargon, you will come across as an insider.

Who are the major players in the industry? Some industries are oligopolies with only two or three players who set the rules of play. Other industries are highly fragmented with no significant players. Who defines the rules of play in the industry you've targeted? How high are the barriers to entry? How easy is it to exit the industry? How intense is the rivalry between players?

Is there impending regulation, or have regulations recently been imposed?

What are the main objectives for the players in the industry? Are they concerned with environmental issues? Are they concerned with unfair trade practices? What about emerging technology?

In addition to the industry, you'll need to do your homework on the company and the individual(s) you'll be meeting.

Who does the organization currently do business with? Who have they done business with in the past? Are there companies they currently do business with that are not competitive? Can you talk to the relevant salespeople to find out more about your target company? Are there any publications online that you can read? It's surprising what you can uncover using Google's file type command in your searching.

If your target company is public, there will be lots of great information available. Pay particular attention to annual reports and, more specifically, to the letter to shareholders. In the letter to shareholders, the CEO will outline the key strategic initiatives of the organization. Please note, however, that this letter is a form of propaganda (i.e., it's designed to promote a biased point of view). Much time and anguish goes into every word in the annual report. Each letter must work vigorously to win the confidence of the shareholders.

Tip: To prevent yourself from being sucked into the emotional journey the authors of the letter want to take you down, read the letter backwards. That's right! Start with the last sentence and read each preceding sentence until you get to the top. This will inoculate you from getting emotionally engaged. If there is any bad news to be reported, it will be buried in the middle of the letter after you've been won over with all the great things that are happening. When you read the letter backward, this bad news will jump off the page because you haven't been sucked in emotionally.

Speaking of emotions, be sure to extract the strategic initiatives from the letter. These initiatives are goals. Emotions are tied to goals. How can you support these goals?

How long has the CEO been on board? If he or she is new, what do they need to correct? More importantly, what was their formula for success at their old company? How can you become part of their trusted advisors to execute their strategies, based on what you know about their formula for success?

When Jay Leno left *The Tonight Show* in 2009 after seventeen years, he provided us with an instructive example of how many CEOs operate. Three months after he graciously handed over the reins to Conan O'Brien, Jay Leno launched his new show on September 14, 2009. Of course, as the master of humor and timing, his debut was not a disappointment—well, not entirely. I have to admit I was a little bit disappointed. I was expecting something new and I thought new meant different.

The Jay Leno Show was not dissimilar from *The Tonight Show*. Jay's loyal sidekick, Kevin Eubanks, also made his debut with The Prime Time Band (different in name only from the Tonight Show Band). On March 1, 2010, Jay Leno resumed his role as host of *The Tonight Show*.

As I processed my disappointment with the apparent lack of creativity, I realized that Jay is the same as CEOs who move from one company to another. After many years, they develop their formula for success. They have a certain way of getting things done that leverages their strengths. They also have a network of close associates whom they trust, who understand them, and whom they can rely on to get things done.

When a CEO moves from one company to another, the strategy he or she will employ to make a mark and put some quick successes on the board is entirely predictable. It will be the same strategy that brought them success in their previous role. In order to execute that strategy, the CEO will need to be surrounded by reliable people. Inevitably, they will recruit their trusted network into the new company in an effort to reduce the number of unknowns associated with their new role.

This is a perfectly reasonable approach except in the following circumstances:

1. The new environment differs significantly from the old one and the strategies that worked well in the old environment are ineffective in the new one. This can be as a result of the strategies being ineffective in the new environment or the strategies violating deep-seated cultural norms or tightly held values.
2. The trusted network that is recruited into the new environment does not have the deep relationships and influence that are needed in the new environment in order to get things done.
3. A competitor understands this tendency and employs a counter-strategy that sets the CEO up for failure.

In addition to the qualitative information in the shareholder's letter, pay attention to the financials. What's most important about the financials is how they trend over time and how they compare to industry norms. Look for line items that differ markedly from industry norms. Also look for how line items are trending. To do this you'll need to do a bit of ratio analysis. Ratios get to the heart of the financial story. They explore profitability, use of assets, debt, and ownership. There are many online resources that will help you understand what the important ratios are and how to calculate them. If you're not comfortable doing the calculations, hire an accountant to do them for you and to help you find where improvement is needed.

Ideally, you can see how your organization can positively impact the financials of your target company. Can you increase sales or cut costs? Can you reduce inventory? Can you speed up collections? Make sure you're clear about your potential impact on the balance sheet, income statement, or cash-flow statement.

Here is some more homework: How is your target company structured? Why is it structured that way? Has it ever been restructured? Why? Remember, structure supports strategy. Note who reports to whom, and ask yourself why they might be structured this way. There are many online resources that can help you with this exercise. Officialboard.com is one of them. Don't forget to check out your local library. Librarians are highly skilled in searching publications and databases that might not be accessible on the Internet. Why not leverage their skills?

At the individual level, what is each contact's educational background? How we are educated shapes our thinking. Engineers think very differently from marketing majors. If you're selling to an engineer, you'd better have your facts and you'd better avoid hyperbole. If you're selling to a marketing professional, you need to be able to see the big picture and be ready to move quickly from one topic to the next. What about their career path? Someone who has come up through operations and now sits in the CEO chair will think very differently from someone who has come up the ranks through sales.

What can you find out about what's motivating your contact to meet with you? Many people are motivated by fixing something that's gone wrong - but not everyone. Some, especially chief executives, are highly motivated by growth and what's possible.

Clarify what additional information you need to uncover and what you want the buyer to do as a result of meeting with them.

Salespeople are paid to influence the decisions of buyers. They are paid to help buyers buy. Buying is an action. In fact, it is the culmination of a series of actions. If someone is buying from you, they are taking action. The effectiveness of each meeting therefore must be measured by the action the buyer has taken as a result of your meeting.

Action is a function of belief. In other words, people behave the way they do because of what they believe. The reason potential buyers are not yet buying from you is they don't really believe buying from you will help them. If they did, they would already be buying from you.

Salespeople must be very clear about what action they expect from the buyer and what belief must be in place for the buyer to take that action. Sales is a series of interactions that continually shift the beliefs of buyers, resulting in a series of actions that ultimately culminates in a purchase.

As you determine what you want the buyer to do as a result of your meeting, consider the following:

1. How many interactions has your firm had with the buyer?
2. Where are they in their buying process?
3. What do you know about their approval process and the key influencers?
4. What are the main concerns the key influencers have?
5. What led up to the current situation, and what is the strategic context?
6. What is the cause and what are the implications of the challenges the buyer is facing?
7. What is the next logical action you can ask the buyer to perform, and what do they need to believe to perform this action?

As you consider what information to uncover, take the time to review your question library. A question library is a checklist of great questions you have in your toolkit to help you structure your sales conversations.

Once you are clear about the action the buyer should take and the supporting belief that is required, you should list all the attendees who will be in the meeting along with their title, organization, and role. Think about where they fit in the organizational structure, what their objectives are, and what their roles are in the meeting. Think about the concerns/issues they might have as a result of their position/ perspective. Craft your agenda to address these issues, and be clear about how you will address or preempt potential issues that might come up.

Next, craft a series of agenda items that will address the key concerns, build the required belief, and end with a request for the buyer to take the desired and logical next action. Both the sequence of topics and desired next step should be spelled out clearly for the buyer. Sales reps are often nervous about doing this because they feel that by being so explicit they run the risk of being rejected. The opposite is true. Senior executives love clarity, and they love to know what people who meet with them are asking them to do. Remember, we are not in the manipulation business. We are in the business of helping people make optimal buying decisions to improve their lives.

Before sharing the agenda with your buyer, your team should ensure they provide context for the meeting. Again, executives are busy and often run from one meeting to another with little or no preparation time. They may have been crystal clear about why they were meeting with you when they booked the appointment, but so much has happened between then and now that they no longer remember the key details or purpose of the meeting. For this reason, you want to put your agenda in context. You do this by stating the purpose for the meeting and its context. This also helps build value if the buyer decides to circulate your agenda to other executives.

List any questions you need answered before going into the meeting. Include these questions along with the anticipated issues you expect to encounter and your planned approach in a meeting plan to be shared internally. Have your peers review your meeting plan and give you feedback prior to sharing your agenda with the buyer.

Finally, send your draft agenda and get feedback and approval from the buyer. Be careful. If the buyer has no changes to make to the agenda, it might mean that he or she is not emotionally engaged in the meeting. The key benefit of sharing the agenda is that you now have agreement on who will participate, what will be covered, the sequence in which it will be covered, and the action you are expecting the decision maker to take at the end of the meeting. This resolves the issue of competing agendas, it enables you to prevent the meeting from being derailed (if anything comes up that is not in the agenda, you can put it in the parking lot), and it enables you to demonstrate leadership to the executive you are selling to.

Executives love to surround themselves with people who can get things done! Remember, preparation is the foundation of leadership.

2. Flawless Execution

Arrive early and start on time! Remember, you are influencing beliefs. If you can't run a meeting on time, how well can you ensure a project runs according to schedule? Doing things on time, every time, builds trust, and trust is the foundation of every sale.

After you exchange pleasantries, place your agenda in front of you so that it is clearly visible to everyone in the meeting. Remind everyone of the purpose of the meeting. Ask if everyone has had a chance to review the agenda and if it's okay for you to begin with the first item on the agenda. By agreeing to address the first item on the agenda, everyone is agreeing to adhere to the agenda items. If anything comes up that is not on the agenda, ask if it's okay to put that in the parking lot. You can cover it at the end of the meeting if there is time, or you can agree to put it on the agenda for your next meeting. Move smoothly from one agenda item to the next. As each agenda item is covered, make careful note of the conclusion that was reached. You will use this as part of your follow-up after the meeting. In the course of the meeting, after you have uncovered the key goals and needs of your buyer, you should share with them how you can help.

3. Effective Follow-up

One of the most effective ways you can build trust is what you do after a meeting. Most salespeople have ineffective follow-up. Professional follow-up will clearly differentiate you from your competitors.

Go back over your agenda and record the decisions reached on each item. Create a schedule of agreed-upon next actions and clearly note the date and time of your next meeting. Send this follow-up within forty-eight hours of your meeting. This will ensure everyone in the meeting agrees on what was accomplished. It will also keep the emotional momentum going in your absence. Finally, it will prompt your prospective client to create a file for your company—a key step in making your company a part of your prospective client's world.

This will feel mentally difficult and possibly awkward the first few times you do it. Thinking clearly is hard work and managing meetings effectively takes effort. However, the payoff will be immediate and rewarding. Very shortly, the process will become habitual and painless and you will have put yourself in the top 1 percent of all the sales interactions your prospective clients have.

CEO Action Plan

- ❏ Ensure your marketing funnel is properly linked to your sales funnel by making marketing responsible for first meetings.
- ❏ Develop a drip marketing campaign to nurture leads that are not ready to buy today.
- ❏ Simplify your sales funnel. Focus on sales phases not steps.
- ❏ Clean out your existing funnel. Don't allow your sales funnel to get clogged with opportunities that are not real.

Sales Professional Action Plan

- ❏ Clean up your sales funnel. Nature hates a vacuum. When you clear out what isn't real, you're making space for what is.
- ❏ Stop cold calling. Figure out how you can become a thought leader and attract leads with value.
- ❏ Start preparing agendas for your meetings. Demonstrate you value the time your prospective clients give to you.

Chapter 3

A-SALE AND A STORY

Storytelling is the most powerful way to put ideas into the world today.
—**Robert McAfee Brown**

E arlier we talked about the importance of understanding the emotions behind why people buy. I've developed a simple methodology to uncover strategic objectives in a meeting and to combine the emotional energy of yearning with the emotional energy of avoidance. I call it A-SALE. A-SALE is an acronym that helps you do two things: 1) uncover the real value of what you are selling and 2) ensure your prospective client is fully engaged emotionally (via approach and avoidance).

Buying is about change, or moving from the current state through a transition state to a future state. The A-SALE method uncovers the current and desired future state by engaging both the reptilian and limbic centers of the brain and is a powerful method to help people buy.

A is for Amenity. The dictionary definition of amenity is the "pleasantness of a place or a person." The purpose of amenity questions is to create a pleasant environment and make the buyer comfortable. This is important because the basic reptilian brain is skittish. It is constantly on alert for danger.

Whenever we meet someone new, they represent a potential threat. If this part of the mind never settles, your meeting will be unproductive. Information will not be freely shared and you could even be given misinformation. In order to create safety, you must first find common ground. Amenity questions boil down to small talk with big implications. When people ask questions like "Isn't it hot?", "Did you catch the game?", "How long have you been here?", and so forth, they are engaging in small talk. Small talk does a couple of things. It allows us to make quick assessments. We can study the amount of eye contact, rate of speech, diction, body movements, etc. All of this data gets processed by the reptilian brain to assess how familiar or strange you are. If you are perceived as familiar, the reptilian brain relaxes. If you are strange, the reptilian brain remains on guard. The reptilian brain is simpleminded. When it finds a couple of familiar data points, it jumps to the conclusion that everything else is familiar.

Within a matter of moments, sufficient rapport can be built up such that two people can feel like they've known each other for a long time. This is the "we" space you want to set up to have substantive conversation.

Our objective with the A-SALE methodology is to engage the limbic and reptilian minds. At the end of the process, we will ask the client to envision a better future. As part of the amenity process, we should plant the seed for what that future might look like. Storytelling serves the dual purpose of creating a safe environment while also planting the seed for the future vision.

S is for Strategic Context. Immediately following the amenity phase, most salespeople want to get down to business. They begin asking questions like "So how long have you been having this problem?" or "What do you think this could be costing you?" These questions are designed to get at the pain in the organization and explore how the sales professional might add value. The problem with asking these questions is that most executives have been around the block (a couple of times) and they know we're asking these questions to figure out how we can make a sale. This realization triggers the reptilian brain to become defensive. All the good work that was done to settle the reptilian brain has suddenly been undone.

Prior to exploring the areas of pain that you can address, I recommend that you spend some time understanding your buyer strategically. Executives are used to starting at the general and working their way to the specific, so this will feel very natural to them. Also, when you ask questions that explore the strategic context of your buyer, the answers do not help you sell anything. This puts the reptilian brain at ease. It perceives that you are trying to understand, not to sell. Everyone longs to be understood. They immediately appreciate you for doing this. As you ask strategically oriented questions, they also begin to perceive you as someone who could serve as a trusted advisor, not just another salesperson.

The strategic objective is the vision in the future that is pulling the organization forward. Remember, people are naturally creative. The strategic objective is formulated using the faculty of imagination. As you align with this vision, you become a valued resource.

Strategic-context questions uncover approach goals. They are thirty-thousand-foot questions that help you understand the big picture. They uncover where the executive is driving his or her organization and the supporting and opposing forces. They should challenge the executive and force him or her to really think. They will appreciate this intellectual stimulation.

While good strategic-context questions will cause the executive to want to use your entire time together discussing these topics, you can't stay at thirty thousand feet. Strategic-context questions don't help you sell anything. They just help you to understand. At some point in the conversation, you need to land the plane in an airport where you can do business.

A is for Attention Focusing. You must now ask questions that enable you to explore how you can help. I call these *attention-focusing questions*. Strategic-context questions are concerned with the future. Attention-focusing questions are concerned with the present and the past. Their purpose is to steer the executive's attention to a specific area of his/her business where you can help. You want to explore what is happening in that area that shouldn't be happening or what isn't happening that should be. You want to explore what led up to this point and what the implications of this issue are. You want to explore the financial consequences. To do this, you must uncover evidence. This is where you get into the nitty-gritty of the problem area.

L is for Linkage. As a result of your investigative attention-focusing questions, you've uncovered their needs and areas of pain. Congratulations! Don't get too comfortable, though. Despite how great you feel about uncovering the pain, it's not enough.

Remember, every business has more needs than it can address. Every business learns to tolerate a certain amount of pain. The longer they live with the pain, the more they realize how much they can live with it. There's a difference between needs and priorities. Needs are real, but priorities are important and must be addressed. Every leader learns to prioritize and to say "no" or "not now" to many needs. They learn to develop a "top ten" list. Things on the list get addressed. Everything else has to wait.

You need to connect the area of need that you've uncovered to the strategic priorities of the business. Actually, you don't need to do this; your buyer needs to do this. You get them to do this by simply asking them to link the area of need to their strategic objectives. This is as simple as saying something like "Earlier we were talking about [strategic objective]. Can you please help me understand how [area of need] connects to [strategic objective]?" That's it. Nothing more! It's important that you don't provide the answer here. The buyer must connect the dots.

As they search for the answer, they'll begin to see the connection. When they do, it will cause a feeling of enlightenment. They'll actually get an emotional charge from realizing the strategic importance of the area of need. When they realize this, the need is promoted to a priority. They see that if the need is left unaddressed, it will compromise their ability to achieve their strategic objective. Immediately, the approach goals and the avoidance goals are combined and interlinked. This creates an emotional charge and generates the emotional energy required to move forward.

E is for Envisioning. The attention-focusing questions uncover problem areas. You don't want to end on a negative note. Envisioning questions are designed to end the conversation on a positive note. These questions must be visually oriented. For example, "Can you please paint a picture for me of what the ideal future looks like if you could eliminate all the issues we discussed?" The visual cues are critical to this question type. You want to encourage the buyer to talk in visual language. You want to see what they see. As they answer the question, they will have to paint a picture for you. When they paint the picture for you, they are really painting it for themselves.

If you did a great job of engaging them with storytelling in the amenity stage, the images they created in their mind will now influence the image they paint as they envision their new future.

As they formulate this new approach goal, they can't help but experience a yearning for it. They see it and they want it! They see it and it excites them. They feel themselves moving toward it. They experience a gap between where they are and where they want to be. They realize you can help them get there, and they want you to help them get there. The positive emotions associated with their vision become attached to you. The meeting now ends on a positive note. It's easy for them to agree to the next step as they see the next step moving them closer to their approach goal.

Here's what an A-SALE conversation might sound like. It's abbreviated, but you'll get an idea of how such a conversation would flow.

Audrey (sales training salesperson): It's great to finally sit down with you Tom. In noticed from your LinkedIn profile, that you've only been at ACME Corp. for a couple of years. How did ACME Corp find you?

Tom (prospective client): My previous boss came here first. He then recruited me. I worked for him for a couple of years and then when he left, I was promoted to VP Sales.

Audrey: Obviously, you're very talented! What stood out for you as significantly different from your previous company when you first started to work here?

Tom: I'd say it's the culture. The culture here is vibrant. People really understand the mission and really apply themselves to its realization.

Audrey: That's excellent! What a wonderful opportunity it must be to work in an environment like this. As I suggested in the agenda that I sent to you last week, I'd like to start our meeting at the 30,000 foot level in order to get a greater appreciation for context. You mentioned the ACME's mission, which I'm familiar with. I wonder if we could spend a few moments discussing your goals for the company for the next 3-5 years.

Tom: Absolutely! It's very simple. The most important thing for us right now is to dominate our market. We need to be number one in this market. There's no reason at all why we should be playing catch up.

Audrey: When we spoke on the phone, you mentioned that you are really pleased with the people you now have on your sales team. Since people don't seem to be the issue, am I correct in assuming that developing the people you have is a priority?

Tom: Yes. We haven't trained our sales people for some time. In fact, I don't think we've ever invested in formal training. We need to do something.

Audrey: Why do you think training is the issue? I mean, what evidence would you point to if I were to push back and say I don't think it's a training issue.

Tom: Well, I'd point to the number of sales we've lost or had to discount in order to win. Our people can be sloppy at times. They can miss doing proper investigation and miss aligning our capabilities with customer priorities. Just last week, Jason came to me all excited about a big deal that was imminent only to tell me this week that we lost it. When I drilled down, some of the fundamentals were missed. We had no right submitting a proposal. It was premature. If we could only get our people and their managers to really understand our points of differentiation and present them clearly, we could do so much better. They need to follow a sound process and not fly by the seat of their pants. Talent is great, but it can be magnified with a strong process.

Audrey: Earlier you mentioned the need to dominate your market. How does sales training address this need?

Tom: We can't afford to lose major accounts. When we get our chance at bat, we've got to hit home runs consistently. There are only so many of these major opportunities that come up each year. We can't afford to strike out. And there's no need for us to strike out. If we can consistently get on base and bring these deals home, we can dramatically shift our position in the marketplace and really get some momentum going.

Audrey: I get it. Sounds great! If I could wave a magic wand and eliminate all the problems you mentioned, how do you see your sales team behaving and what do you see in terms of how your market would respond?

One of our clients is WBM Office Systems in western Canada. They are one of Canada's top 50 largest IT solution providers. The President, JoeAnne Hardy and the Vice President, Brett Bailey wanted to elevate the level of engagement they had with their customers. We worked with their sales team to help them master the A-SALE discovery process. They typically sell to very large corporations. Using A-SALE as a framework for C-suite conversations, they have steadily engaged the most senior executives in their market. In a short time, they have become a regional powerhouse and have developed an enviable reputation as the go to resource for CIOs in western Canada. In the time since they have adopted this process, their company has grown dramatically and their sales team has more than tripled in size.

If you'd like a copy of some sample A-SALE questions, go to http://adriandavis.com/Free-Resources and look in the Free Resources section.

The Defining Metaphor

One more thing: throughout the A-SALE process, listen carefully for metaphors. Metaphors are at the root of our communications. Whenever we use one thing to represent another, we are using metaphor. Metaphor is at the root of learning. Metaphors also represent shorthand. A picture paints a thousand words, and a metaphor can capture a thousand years (e.g., the Dark Ages). As you listen to your buyers, listen for what I call the *defining metaphor*. Inevitably, whether it's during the strategic context, attention focusing, or envisioning segment of the conversation, you'll eventually hear the metaphor that captures the essence of what is happening or needs to happen.

The defining metaphor captures all of the history associated with the problem and simplifies it for the reptilian brain where it can be stored. All interactions are then pegged against the defining metaphor. Learn to listen for this metaphor and articulate your value by extending the metaphor. When you do this, you will connect at a very deep level with your buyer.

Here are some sample defining metaphors you might hear alongside some examples of how you could position your value to connect to the metaphor.

Metaphor	Proposal Title
"Stuck in the mud"	Getting Unstuck and in High Gear
"Stuck in neutral"	Moving into Overdrive
A deep groove	A Smooth Transition to Massive Progress
Foot on the gas and brake at the same time	Gaining Traction toward Major Success
Spinning our wheels	

Storytelling

Salespeople are educators. The typical salesperson spends a lot of time learning about his or her company and its products and services. Unfortunately, much of this effort is a waste of time. It's a waste of time because buyers today are very sophisticated. Most of them do lots of research before ever reaching out to a vendor. By the time they contact you, they're very educated on what your company does and what it provides. As a result, the typical salesperson's presentation is perceived as redundant and a waste of time.

As you present your information to a potential buyer, on the surface they may appear engaged, but on the inside they are often bored and highly critical.

People want to be engaged. They want to be interested. They want to believe.

We need to change our approach.

Let's cut back on the PowerPoint and the facts and figures and begin to tell stories. Stories are incredibly powerful. Human beings are wired for story—for hearing stories and for telling them. Story is how we make sense of the world around us. Stories contain meaning and morals. They contain experiences and explanations. We are where we are today because of the power of story. From an early age we learned to pay attention whenever someone began to tell us a story. That engaged us. Even today a curious part of us comes back to life whenever we listen to a story.

A story has a beginning, a middle, and an end. Once you begin, you create a gap until you reach the conclusion. Our minds hate gaps. We pay attention until the very end until the gap is closed. We also know there may be twists and turns through the middle, so we can't jump to conclusions. The critical thinking faculty is put on hold until the end. This means that when we tell a good story, it goes straight into the hearts and minds of our listeners without interference. It's accepted in its entirety before it's unpacked and evaluated.

In the middle, there must be a point of conflict. An obstacle is overcome. A villain is vanquished. This is what gives the story meaning. As a result of the resolution of this conflict, something changes. A person matures. A company is transformed. The day is saved.

There are two types of stories we must tell as sales professionals.

1. Your Story of Origin

The first is our story of origin. Whenever we meet someone and we try to engage them to buy something from us, they want to know why we are in the business we are in. Is this something we just fell into the day before we met them to make a quick dollar, or does what we're doing have meaning to us? Our story of origin answers this question and gives us the voice of authenticity. I love teaching others how to be successful in sales because it was my sales career that enabled me to turn my life around. I've spent my entire adult life studying the science of sales. Sales is not something I fell into after having another career. It is what I fell in love with while in college and specifically set out to master. I've been incredibly successful in my own career and in helping others with their sales success. When I show up to help an individual or organization with their sales challenges, my story of origin gives me credibility and authenticity. My passion for sales makes it clear to them that I want them to win. I don't hide the fact that I want to win too. If it's not win-win, I'm not interested. When crafting your story of origin, answer the following questions:

1. How did you get into the business?
2. Why did you get into the business?
3. What success have you had?
4. Why is it fulfilling to you?
5. What's in it for you?

The answer to the last question is especially important. People need to know what your motive is. If you leave them guessing, you erode trust.

2. The Hero's Journey

You need to tell stories about your success. When telling your success stories, be careful not to make yourself the hero. If you do, you'll appear boastful and you'll alienate your buyer. Be sure to make your customer the hero. By extension, you're a hero too. You're the one who intervened and saved the day, but it's your customer that got the promotion, made the deal, or saved costs as a result.

Telling the Hero's Journey involves five steps.

THE HERO'S JOURNEY

1. Introduce hero
2. Hero meets villain
3. Acquires new resource
4. Struggle / triumph
5. Transformation

Figure 5.1. The Hero's Journey

1. Introduce the hero. The hero should be similar to your listener in role and goal. When I hear the story of someone in a similar role to me, I can't help but listen. Remember, stories are how we learn to navigate our world. Any story about someone in a similar role goes into my database for future reference. If I find myself in a similar situation, I will draw on my story database to figure out what I should do. The hero should also have a similar goal. Our emotional system is tied to goals. When you tell me about someone who accomplished something similar to what I'm trying to accomplish, you not only have my undivided attention, you have also switched me on emotionally. As you begin your story, I subconsciously enter into the skin of your hero, and I experience everything your hero experiences in the story.

All of us have mirror neurons that turn on when we see someone experience something. In a very real sense, we feel a bit of what they are feeling. Neuroscience shows that the very same synapses that fire in the victim or the hero fire in us as we watch. Letting the customer be the hero is critical because potential clients will put themselves in the story and see themselves as the hero. This is empowering. This stirs the emotions and agitates us to action. This generates the beliefs and the will to do something—to take action. If you make yourself the hero, your potential client will not relate in the same way. You're a potential supplier; why would they relate to you? They will, however, immediately relate to your customers who faced similar situations.

2. Next, introduce the villain. The hero must be a person, but the villain can be a person, place, or thing. The hero must be a person in order to trigger empathy. Be careful not to make the hero a company. We really don't care about companies. We care about people. When the hero confronts the villain, you will trigger suspense and concern. Because I am in the skin of your hero and I understand what he or she is trying to accomplish, I understand what is at stake when the villain appears.

As a result of the villain's presence, the hero experiences setbacks. Things go from bad to worse. As I listen I can't help but feel defeat. I also experience hope and suspense because you wouldn't be telling me this story if there wasn't a happy ending. I can't help but wonder what happens next to get the hero out of his or her trouble. The trouble the hero encounters also acts as a veiled threat. Because the hero is in a similar circumstance to me, the fact that he/she experiences such setbacks indicates to me that the same could happen to me. This realization helps me feel less attached to my status quo and gets me in a place where I can begin to entertain a new future.

3. This is where you come in. You're not the hero. You're the new resource that the hero accesses. You're like the sword that the hero uses to slay the dragon. You provide the missing piece of wisdom that the hero needed in order to stop spinning his/her wheels. You simply explain the "coincidence" that occurred for you and the hero to meet. How the hero explained to you what they were facing and how you understood and helped.

It's important that you don't steal the show here. Remember, you're not the hero. As a result of working with you, the hero was able to accomplish more. You're a resource, nothing more. Every hero needs resources to accomplish their goal. With the new resource, the hero is able to fight back successfully.

4. Here the hero experiences triumph. By extension, your buyer experiences triumph and has vicariously purchased your services.

5. As a result of the triumph, the hero and/or the hero's world is transformed. This is the critical part of the story. People buy results. This part of the story enables you to showcase the results you can provide. People buy change. Change is about going from current state through a transition state to a future better state. The transition state is a cost. It is a sacrifice, but it's a sacrifice one is willing to make if it brings about a better state. Ideally, the hero is the one who gets transformed in the process. There is some new learning or development as a result of the process. At the very least, the hero's world is transformed in some meaningful way.

Remember, action is a function of belief. Beliefs are built on experiences. These experiences don't have to be our own. We can learn from other people's experiences. In fact, we need to learn from other people's experiences. Are you ready to share your stories?

The combination of great stories and great questions will do wonders to engage and agitate the emotions of your potential buyers.

To recap, there are two types of stories you must learn to tell. The first is your Story of Origin—the story of how you got into the business. It's what gives you credibility. I should have a sense that your work is really meaningful to you when I hear your Story of Origin. The second is the Hero's Journey. This is the story of how you have helped your customers. In this story, they are the hero, not you. As you cast your customer in the role of a hero, I come to understand how I can be a hero.

You can access templates and examples for these story types at http://adriandavis.com/Free-Resources in the Free Resources section.

A final word on storytelling: I'm often asked if one can stretch the truth in stories to make a greater emotional impact. The answer is NO. There are stories you can tell that are passed down from generation to generation, and each time the story is told the storyteller takes the liberty to alter the details to suit his/her purposes. The storyteller does so without violating the fundamental truth of the story. This works because the listeners understand the story is a legend, and while some details may be made up, the kernel of truth in the story is sacred. In terms of storytelling for sales, the entire story must be accurate. Salespeople have a bad reputation to begin with. If you deviate from the truth, you will destroy trust. Don't worry about the emotional impact. It will happen. Just tell your story and use the five-step process outlined above. The emotional impact happens at a subconscious level.

Next Steps

After the discovery and storytelling portions of your meeting, discuss how you might work together and then agree on next steps. At the conclusion of the meeting, state what you believe you've accomplished together, what action items have been agreed to, and confidently ask for the specific action the meeting was set up to accomplish. For example, "I think this has been a very productive meeting. I feel that I'm very clear on your objectives. In terms of next steps, you're going to email me the sample reports by Friday and I'm going to get in touch with your direct reports and schedule meetings with them within two weeks. After meeting with them, we'll meet again and I'll debrief my findings with you. Since we're both busy, why don't we go ahead and schedule our next meeting when we can review my findings together? Do you have your calendar handy?"

If your prospective client is seriously considering using your services to solve their problem, they will continue to set aside time to meet with you. The moment your prospective client no longer wishes to schedule you in their calendar, you are on shaky ground. They are no longer trading their currency of time for your value. It's unlikely they will trade money if they are unwilling to trade time.

Reach versus Richness

Wouldn't you agree that not all prospective clients are equal and not all clients are equal? If that is true, then why do so many companies only have one sales process? Having only one sales process means you are most likely lavishing too much attention on most of your prospective clients and not enough on others. I recommend companies have two processes.

The first is a relatively "lite" process that focuses on reaching as many qualified prospective clients as possible and shepherding them through their buying process. In this process, many of the touch points are automated yet personalized.

Second, companies should also invest in a comprehensive "rich" process for highly qualified prospective clients (and current clients) that will result in strategic, high-value engagements. This process should be reserved for your best opportunities (i.e., the 20 percent that will yield 80 percent of your business). The key to the richness process is that it is highly strategic and requires an investment of time by your brightest resources. The key to the success of this process is the information you gather to create strategic value. Due to the investment required to do this properly, you can't afford to treat all prospective clients equally. Minimizing time spent on "reach" prospective clients enables you to focus on "richness" prospective clients.

However, given the softness of the economy, you can't afford to ignore "reach" prospective clients. Some of them will become "rich" clients, and having lots of them keeps the cash flowing. You need both reach and richness in your sales methodology, and you need to excel at both. It can be done with the right design and forethought, and the rewards are immense.

CEO Action Plan

- ☐ Commission a neutral third party to interview your clients and find out what benefits they are experiencing as a result of your company's intervention.
- ☐ Bring your sales, marketing, and service teams together and brainstorm on your customer successes.
- ☐ Develop a centrally located story database and question library.

Sales Professional Action Plan

- ☐ Interview your clients and find out what happened before, during, and after they implemented your solution. Get details. Find out what went wrong and what went right.
- ☐ Begin crafting your story of origin.
- ☐ Begin crafting a library of "hero's journey" stories and share them immediately. Practice at home first. Watch for reactions. Do people want to know more?
- ☐ Begin categorizing your stories based on role and goal of the hero.
- ☐ Start asking better questions.
- ☐ Access the Question Library and Storytelling Templates in the free resource library at http://adriandavis.com/Free-Resources.

Chapter 4

PHASE TWO: ASSESSMENT

The price of anything is the amount of life you exchange for it.
—**Henry David Thoreau**

T o return to our marriage metaphor, once singles have become "available," the next step is the dating phase. The culmination of the dating phase ends in engagement, the marriage proposal— and ultimately a yes or no. Put simply, Assessment is the buyer's dating phase that will culminate in an accepted proposal. Once buyers begin to explore their options, they look for the best solution and verbally commit. Here are the key attributes of the Assessment phase:

Buyer State of Mind: The buyer has been agitated by fear and/or desire and feels a strong impulse to act. Their logical mind is engaged to try to avoid making a mistake.

Buyer Objectives: During this stage of the buying process, the buyer explores options to close the gap between where they are and where they want to be. You are but one of several alternatives. It would be irresponsible for a buyer to proceed without understanding their options. The impulse to act bubbles up from the reptilian and limbic systems and awakens and engages the cortex. The assessment phase is governed by the logical mind; however, it's important to remember that it is fueled by the emotional mind.

Salesperson's Objectives: The buyer's objective is to choose the best option from competing alternatives. It's important to note, however, that in the Awareness phase the buyer identified a gap between where they are and where they want to be. Remember, the brain hates gaps. When we see gaps we immediately fill them. This insight means buyers enter the Assessment phase with a solution in mind. The mental purchase is made in the Awareness phase. It's critical to understand that you are working in the Assessment phase either to protect or displace a mental purchase made in the Awareness phase.

Another key objective in this phase is to gather the quantifiable information necessary to cost-justify the solution. This will be a critical component of the proposal later in the process.

Risks

- The seller is not clear on the decision criteria and allows another vendor to more effectively address them.
- There isn't sufficient emotional energy for the buyer to complete the buying cycle after getting through the logical Assessment phase.
- The salesperson cuts corners and is unable to provide the logical support the buyer needs to justify the purchase to him/herself and others.
- The seller does not treat this phase as mutual and enters into a subordinate relationship with the buyer.
- The salesperson fails to understand the buyer's internal culture and processes and is unable to help the buyer navigate the purchasing decision for approval.

Logical Support

Old-school "product-push" selling focuses on how to close the sale. Helping buyers *buy* shifts the focus from closing to opening. How you open the sales dialog defines the sale. Gaps are recognized, acknowledged, and closed in the Awareness phase. If you're first in, the buyer has mentally bought your offer in order to mentally close the recognized gap. Your work in the Assessment phase is to provide the logical justification to support and reinforce this decision.

In order to engage in the phase successfully, you must be clear about what business you are in. You will excel in this phase if you excel at relationship building. You'll excel at relationship building if you are doing more than chasing transactions. Are you in the transaction business or the transformation business?

If you are in the transaction business, what happens after someone buys from you doesn't concern you. You're happy to have the benefit of the transaction. Even transactional businesses understand that they must invest in relationship building. However, they do so reluctantly.

If you are in the transformation business, you are committed to the improvement of your client's life. You are committed to the results the client experiences and you naturally invest in building relationships.

Transaction focus keeps you at the supplier stage. Transformation focus propels you into the trusted advisor and symbiotic partner stages.

When you operate as a trusted advisor or symbiotic partner, you operate as a consultant first and a vendor second. Much of the work you do as a consultant you will not directly get paid for. The transactions will come later, and this is how and when you'll get paid. The work you do is transformative. The way you get paid is through transactions. Two metrics that will help your organization support your investment in relationship building are customer lifetime value (LTV) and customer acquisition cost (CAC).

Unless you understand what the value of a customer is over the lifetime of the customer relationship, you will resist investing in the customer acquisition process. When buyers reach out to you, you must be prepared to differentiate yourself from all the other vendors that are calling on them.

Generally speaking, it's in the Assessment phase that the buyer reaches out to vendors and invites them in to explain how they can address the identified challenge. If you're not the vendor who brought them into a state of awareness, the worst thing you can do is engage in the assessment process. Why? Because buying is rooted in emotional agitation, not logical analysis. Logical analysis is an inhibitory response. It's designed to prevent us from making a mistake. If you are second or third to the party, the buyer is emotionally engaged to someone else and is looking for reasons to support the decision they've already made in the Awareness phase.

The first one to the party is usually seen as the trusted advisor and gets to help set out the framework within which the evaluation of all solutions will take place. It is highly likely if you're not first to the party that your solution is being evaluated against criteria that do not put you in the best light. While you think you are showing your best features, the buyer is missing them and recording your shortcomings.

Buyers will only recognize the features of your product or service that resonate with the images they already have in their mind. As you discuss or demonstrate your capabilities, these capabilities must be recognized as resources that will enable buyers to get closer to the goals they see in their mind's eye. This underlines why the A-SALE and story processes are so important. They help build images in the mind of the buyer that will trigger a recognition response as you discuss or demonstrate your capabilities.

If your buyer is not emotionally engaged, you need to take them back to the awareness phase. In this case, the mentally selected solution is providing relief from the pain of the actual status quo. Consequently, it represents a type of new mental status quo. You not only have to compete with the actual status quo, you must also displace the new mental status quo. You must expand the awareness of their challenges and create a gap between their actual status quo and their mental status quo and a new desired state. This one step will do more to increase your sales than most sales training programs.

Once emotional engagement is confirmed, you are ready to provide logical support for the emotional decision they've made.

At the end of this process, the buyer wants to come to several logical conclusions. These are:

- We understand what is required.
- What is required is important enough to our business for us to invest in it.
- Any outside vendors who get involved are credible, experienced, and understand what is required for us to be successful.

Critical Skills in the Assessment Phase

The sales professional should not assume that the buyer or seller fully understand the issues. While the buyer is assessing the potential vendor, the vendor should also be assessing the buyer and the buyer's situation. The Assessment phase should be mutual.

Ideally, the salesperson's discovery should be deep and wide. If you engaged the C-level executive properly, he or she has given you permission to do further investigation. Your investigation must do three things:

1. Uncover the underlying issues from multiple perspectives that will drive change
2. Gain agreement on what is really needed
3. Uncover objective, numerical evidence to justify the investment in change

1. Uncover the underlying issues

I often help my clients select software to better run their businesses. And I am often evaluating CRM solutions. It never ceases to amaze me how quickly vendors want to rush to their demonstration and how they frame it with a "brief" PowerPoint presentation. The slide deck typically follows this format:

- How long we've been in business
- What makes us different
- How many customers we have
- How fast we are growing
- Why you need us

The fifth point is often boilerplate and not customized to our client's specific needs. The three or four points they present on the need for their product are generic. They show the same points to every company. The extent of customization of the slide deck is placing our client's logo on the title page.

This behavior is as true of the big players as it is of the small players. It's based on product push, not buyer pull. If you are willing to do your homework and be a consultant first—regardless of what you are selling—you will significantly differentiate yourself from your competitors.

What the product-push perspective fails to understand is that emotion is rooted in goals. Presentations that start with the buyer's specific goals will be far more engaging than presentations that start with boilerplate information on your credentials.

2. Gain agreement on what is needed

Next, you need to summarize what the key issues are that need to be addressed. The only way you can do this succinctly is if you have done your homework to understand all the issues and how they connect, and then distilled them down to the core issues based on the strategic goals of the organization you are selling to.

3. Uncover objective, numerical evidence to justify the investment in change

During your Assessment phase, you want to meet with all the stakeholders. During these meetings, dig into what is happening that shouldn't be happening and what is not happening that should be. While you are uncovering these issues, you also need to uncover the tangible benefits your solution can bring them. You do this by uncovering the specifics of the problem to be addressed. For example, your conversation may uncover the fact that your prospective client's invoices often go out incorrectly. Don't stop there. Find out how many invoices go out each month. What percentage of these invoices contains errors? How much time is added to the collection period as a result? What's the size of the average invoice? How many people process invoices? How much are they paid?

It's important that you do not assume the answers to these questions. You must uncover the actual data. Why? Because you will aggregate this information with all the other information you uncover in all the other departments. You will use this information to calculate what not addressing this issue is costing them. These costs will fall into one of three areas:

1. Increase revenue (opportunity cost)
2. Reduce or eliminate actual costs
3. Avoid future costs

What operational metrics can your solution impact? What is the baseline of these metrics before your intervention, and how long will it take before there is noticeable improvement? If you are thorough in your work, this will be a significant number, and it will be based in the facts the buyer and their stakeholders gave you. From this number you can calculate a return on investment, a payback period, and the daily cost of delaying the decision. This information is very meaningful if your buyer is emotionally engaged and looking for solid support to defend their decision to move forward.

In addition to the tangible benefits, be sure to capture the intangible benefits. Chief executives are often far more interested in the intangible benefits (e.g., improving goodwill with customers, enhancing the power of the brand, etc.), but you must show tangible benefits if you want everyone aligned with the need for your solution.

Your people can't just sell hopes and dreams in today's tough economic climate. Your interventions must be real and measurable. I leave you with a thought that a consultant I respect shared with me: "If we can't express what we know in the form of numbers, we really don't know much about it. If we don't know much about it, we can't control it. If we can't control it, we are at the mercy of chance." I'll add: if we are at the mercy of chance, why do anything different?

The quantifiable information you gather will all be reflected in the proposal you submit. When you look at the proposals your people submit, how clearly are the metrics they will impact reflected? If there are no clear metrics, there probably isn't a clear understanding of what your solution will actually do for your prospective client. The result? An emphasis on features or shallow promises.

Ask your people to slow down, understand the key metrics they can impact, and reflect that understanding in their proposals.

Demonstrations

If you sell a product that must be demonstrated, you are probably demonstrating it too early in the buying process. Buyers want demos right away, but this desire should not be satisfied. A premature demo doesn't do anyone any good. Think of your demo as proof. In fact, whenever you hear the word *demo*, replace it with the word *proof*. When I used to sell CRM software, I would demonstrate the software to try to generate interest. Since I didn't really understand what was needed, I ended up trying to demonstrate everything in the hope that something would capture their interest.

For some reason, and I don't remember why, I left my laptop in my car and went to a meeting with nothing but a pen and notebook. I listened and took good notes. Since I didn't have my laptop with me, the buyer didn't ask for a demo. We agreed to schedule a demo in the next meeting. When I did the demo, I was able to demonstrate how our software could meet their needs. The demo was simple, short, and far more compelling. This was a turning point in my career. Later, I would sell far more complex software that required a technical engineer, but I learned to use these resources carefully and in a very targeted way. Paradoxically, the less software I demonstrated, the larger the deal I ended up writing. In one case, I managed to avoid a demo altogether. I used a well-timed visit to a client site as proof that we could do what we said we could do.

Proposing Solutions

When I ask salespeople to define a proposal, I get all kinds of answers. That explains why most proposals are a big waste of time and effort. They are often bloated and delay sales rather than accelerate sales.

Very simply, a proposal is a request from one party to another to take a specific course of action. When I proposed to my wife, my proposal was a simple question: "Will you marry me?" I was asking her if she would take a particular course of action. The answer was either yes or no. Fortunately for me, the answer was yes! When my wife said yes, it didn't surprise me. If she had said no, I would have been shocked. Our relationship had developed to the point where marriage was the next natural step.

When the proposal is submitted, it should not come as a surprise. The true proposal statement should be a single sentence. This usually gets a strong reaction from salespeople. They get excited and try to explain that their proposals have to be tens, and sometimes hundreds, of pages because of the technical detail that's required. At this point I insist that the proposal is a single sentence, and until they understand this their proposals will continue to be cloudy and prevent action rather than facilitate it.

In addition to the single proposal statement, there are a few other essential elements of a proposal document. Most proposals start with some weak statement about how happy and grateful the supplier is to have a chance to submit the proposal. Several pages of self-indulgence expressing how great the vendor is then follow this weak opening. Combined, these elements put the buyer to sleep. We need to structure the elements of our proposals in a way that awakens the buyer, keeps them engaged, and builds emotional momentum.

Generally speaking, nothing interests buyers more than themselves. Instead of competing with this natural self-interest, work with it. Open your proposal with a statement acknowledging what they've done well to date, what they want to accomplish next, and the challenges standing in their way. What important achievements have they made? What are they trying to accomplish strategically? What is it that they need and why?

These statements should not be more than a couple of paragraphs. They should be concise and strike right at the heart of the matter. Embedded in these statements should be your understanding of the decision criteria your buyer has told you they will use to filter solutions. Each criterion is rooted in a real need, and you must clearly demonstrate how you address these criteria.

When reiterating your buyer's challenges, it's important that you demonstrate a deep grasp of the challenges. Simply repeating what your buyer has told you doesn't demonstrate this. You want to demonstrate that you have digested and processed what they have told you. Typically, the earlier you are engaged in helping your buyer face an emerging challenge, the more likely you are to hear the buyer's needs as a stream of consciousness. I highly recommend that you take everything you've learned and categorize it using a mind map or an outliner. Categories can include symptoms, root causes, past, present, future, etc.

If your potential client is reading your proposal in front of you, you should see their head nodding yes as they read this section. They should feel like you have clearly articulated their current state and requirements clearly, which you discovered during the first meetings, particularly if you used the methods of A-SALE and storytelling we covered in the previous chapter. Your objective is to make them feel understood. The purpose of this section is to engage the reptilian and limbic systems. When their head nods while reading this section, it is unconscious. It is their reptilian brain that feels cared for that is nodding their head. At the end of this section, the reptilian brain is thinking "Right on!" Then it immediately thinks, "Okay. You understand. Now what do we do to fix this?"

That's when your proposal comes in. The next line after you have clearly stated their need should be "In order to meet these needs, I propose that you...." Or, "In order to address these requirements, I recommend that you...." You want to link their needs to your directive. They are vulnerable. You must demonstrate leadership here. You must outline the course of action you want them to take in a clear and succinct manner. This is the key. Executives love being told what's wrong and what they should do about it. Most people just tell them what's wrong. After reading your summary of their need, your proposal statement comes as a relief. The need is the gap; the proposal is how they fill the gap. Remember, your proposal is a single sentence in the form of a directive to which they can respond yes or no.

Once they are clear on the solution, they will want to know your methodology. How will you actually get this done? How much will it cost? How long will it take? Who needs to be involved? What is their investment in time, money, and required resources? Change is about going from current state to a future state through a transition state. Your methodology is your buyer's transition state. This state represents uncertainty, unfamiliarity, and risk. The clearer you are with your methodology, the less fearful your buyer will be about entering this transition state. Many sales are stalled because the buyer feels uncertain about the transition state.

Answer all of these questions as succinctly as possible. Be sure that your answers address their decision criteria. Be precise and concise. If you are selling solutions that are highly technical and require hundreds of pages to explain, think of your traditional proposal as an appendix and think of what you'd typically call the transmission letter or the executive summary as the real proposal. The real proposal document should be no more than two pages and it should be emotional. The methodology section is the one part of your proposal that slows the emotional momentum. It engages the logical mind and addresses risk. Don't get bogged down with too much detail here. Your objective is to give your buyer clarity. If at all possible, use a diagram to introduce this section. Let your buyer see your methodology so that as they read the various sections, they can visually map where each piece fits. Summarize your methodology and refer to an appendix if you require significant technical detail. Your two-page proposal is what will get circulated to the executive team. Your two-hundred-page technical appendix will get circulated to technical staff. That's the way you want it.

The next paragraph should outline the outcomes they will enjoy as a result of adopting your solution. Your objective here is to paint a picture that your buyer can see and that now appears achievable. If this section is done correctly, their reptilian brain can imagine the future in contrast to the current state outlined in your first few paragraphs.

The emotional agitation you've stimulated with the clear statement of the gap, the clear statement of how to fill the gap, and the clear statement of what filling the gap will look like must now be brought to focus on one single sentence. That sentence is the next action. What do you want them to do next? Should they sign an agreement? Prepare a deposit check? Schedule a kickoff meeting? Whatever it is, make it simple and clear. Ultimately, they may have to take ten thousand steps to get there, but that is not important now. What's important now is that they get started.

The mind is funny. Once it gets started on something, it wants to stay with it until it's completed. My son will sometimes ask me if I have a minute to look at something. An hour later, I'm wondering what I was doing before I got interrupted. You want to take all of the emotional energy you've stimulated and point it to a single action that will get them started. The buyer will feel relief from this pent-up energy by taking that first step. And that first step must feel easy. Simply say something like "In order to get started, please...."

The key is to get them started. Many software companies understand this and are now offering their software for a limited time at no charge. They understand that once you get started, inertia will work in their favor. Think about how you can minimize risk and get your prospective client started. If they will just take that first step, it's highly likely that they will continue the journey.

It is important that this request come after the emotional buildup and that the request is clear and immediately actionable. Don't mix the elements. Start with a clear statement of what they need, a clear statement of your proposal, your methodology (i.e., your process to get them through the transition state and their investment of time, money,, and resources), the future state they will enjoy, and then a request for a single next action.

One final word about the elements of your proposal. Don't underestimate the role of the proposal's title. The title is the first thing your buyer will read. When you engaged in the A-SALE dialog, you uncovered what I call the *defining metaphor*. It is the image your buyer uses to articulate their situation. Use that metaphor in your proposal title, but extend it so the title reflects the solution. For example, if the defining metaphor is "our sales engine is sluggish," "Accelerating the Sales Engine" would be an appropriate title. Using the defining metaphor as the title engages and excites the reptilian brain before they even begin reading. Everything looks and feels better when anticipation is switched on.

Engaging the reptilian and limbic systems creates buyer-pull. Buyer-pull is how we overcome the traditional product-push selling, which is irresponsible and self-serving. When buyer-pull is turned on, buyers will proactively seek out the supporting facts of your product or service. The power of this approach lies in how the human mind works: this approach satisfies the prefrontal cortex, limbic, and reptilian parts of the mind. Try it and see how much more quickly your proposals get acted on.

CEO Action Plan

❏ Ensure your sales team carefully selects high-value prospective clients, and help them get the resources they need to do the necessary preparation before a sales call.

❏ Help your team understand how CEOs perceive value as if you were the client.

❏ Ensure all proposals that are issued are clear and that there is sufficient emotional momentum to move to implementation of your solution.

Sales Professional Action Plan

❏ Ensure you are clear on the decision criteria before you present your solution or submit a proposal.

❏ Select high-stakes prospective clients carefully and then set the time aside to do the necessary preparation and follow-up.

❏ Ensure you are in alignment with the buyer's emotions before using logical support materials.

Chapter 5

PHASE THREE: APPREHENSION

There are more things to alarm us than to harm us,
and we suffer more often in apprehension than reality.
—Seneca

B ack to our couple, who is now engaged to be married. Now that they are engaged, the doubts begin. We all know the stereotype of the bride or groom who get "cold feet" just before the wedding. These doubts are actually a natural and healthy process. Each begins seriously thinking about this person as a lifelong companion; they check out their family and their background and are not necessarily pleased with what they discover. They may wonder, *Are they holding things back?* Whereas in the dating phase each person was enamored with the best aspects of the other, once the couple is engaged, very often they begin looking for what's wrong. They're assessing risk.

In the buying cycle, this is called the Apprehension phase. The buyer may not be considering a commitment quite as long-term as marriage, but similarly, once the "best" alternative is selected, the buyer immediately begins to consider the risks associated with the chosen alternative. They imagine all the things that could go wrong. Whereas in the Assessment phase buyers are preoccupied with the best features that led them to accept a proposal, in this stage they're preoccupied with the worst. The status quo begins to appear attractive again. So the buyer needs to reassure him or herself that they are in fact making the right decision and, should the risks begin to unfold, they have a sound strategy to deal with these risks. Here's what this phase looks like at a glance:

Buyer State of Mind: The buyer is agitated by anxiety and feels a strong impulse to revert to the status quo. They need reassurance that they understand the risks and that proceeding is the right decision.

Buyer Objectives: Having confirmed in their mind that your solution is the right one, the buyer now becomes concerned with risk. Their mind becomes flooded with all the things that could go wrong. They are seeking reassurance that the project will unfold as planned and they will achieve the outcomes promised.

Salesperson's Objectives: Most salespeople panic when they feel the buyer begin to back up and express doubts. Rather than panic, you should relax. Why? First, it's the confirmation you are looking for that the buyer has in fact chosen you. Second, if there is sufficient trust in the relationship, the buyer will be willing to share their concerns with you. Your objective in this phase is to uncover the risks and help the buyer mitigate these risks.

Risks

- The seller has not built up sufficient trust for the buyer to share concerns.
- The seller rushes to cover up the concerns instead of exploring and fully understanding them.
- The seller takes ownership of the concerns and commits to fixing everything instead of helping the buyer figure out how they will mitigate the risks and how the seller can help.

Will-Not Power

We've all heard of willpower, but very few of us stop to consider the force of "will-not" power. Our will-not power prevents us from engaging in detrimental activities. It's something we developed with the help of our parents. We learned that not everything we want to do is good to do. We learned to consider the future consequences of our actions, and we developed the power to resist our impulses.

The power to resist based on the consideration of future consequences is an intellectual power. Without our will-not power, we would be in serious trouble.

Willpower is different. Willpower is rooted in emotional agitation. When our emotions are stirred up sufficiently so as to leave us feeling unsettled, we formulate the will to act in a manner that will bring us back to emotional equilibrium.

All progress depends on emotional agitation. On a personal level, the desire to act must be greater than the force not to act. On a corporate level, not only must the individual's "will" overpower their "will-not," it must also overpower the organization's status quo and all the strings that are attached to the status quo.

Whenever change occurs to the status quo, there are winners and losers. Those who perceive themselves as losing will fight hard for the maintenance of or a return to the status quo. Yet every day change happens and progress occurs. This is because of an innate desire in all of us to improve our condition. No matter where we are, we are wired to try to do better.

More often than not, it is the chief executive who is driving the organization to a new future state and who is unwilling to allow things to remain as they are. More often than not, salespeople are selling below the C-suite, and they are selling their firm's capabilities with arguments that appeal to logic and intellect. Instead of selling high and engaging in the emotional reasons for change, they are selling low, engaging that part of the organization that wants to protect the status quo, and appealing to that part of the mind that is responsible for the power of will-not and not the force of will.

Remember, where there's a will, there's a way—unless of course there's a stronger will-not!

Recruiting the Whole Mind

Just because the will to purchase comes from emotional agitation doesn't mean we can ignore the intellect. We still have to sell to the intellect because the buyer must have sound, logical reasons for proceeding. In a business-to-business context, the logical justification needs to boil down to improving the buyer's financial condition. Profitability is the fundamental metric of business. Ultimately, our interventions should result in increased profitability for our clients.

Our impact will either affect the balance sheet or the income statement. We can:

- Increase assets
- Reduce liabilities
- Increase revenues
- Decrease costs
Avoid future costs

Getting from purchasing your product or service to understanding your impact on their financial statements isn't necessarily obvious. If you leave this to your buyer, the connection might never be made. Making this connection is critical when your buyer experiences apprehension. Change is about moving from a current state through a transition state to a future state. The transition state represents the required investment. The future state is the return on that investment. The cost and hassle of going through the transition state is viewed relative to the magnitude of the future state. The more clearly the magnitude of the return is understood, the more motivated the buyer will be to go through the transition state. The more clearly everyone in the buying committee can understand the magnitude of the future state, the easier it will be to gain agreement to proceed with your proposal.

The financial data to cost-justify your solution should be gathered during the mutual Assessment phase. While your buyer is trying to understand your solution, you should be seeking to better understand your buyer's situation. As you perform your discovery to better understand your buyer's challenges and needs, you should be uncovering financial data as well. Seek to quantify any and all problems and needs. You may have a solution that can increase the life of a particular piece of equipment. If that's the case, you need to find out: How many pieces of this equipment does the buyer have? How much does it cost to replace the equipment? Will there be retraining involved with the new equipment? What about shipping and implementation costs? How much life is left in the equipment? By how much can you extend it?

I recommend you have your sales team take a worksheet with them when they are investigating needs. As they investigate each need, they should be diligent to note which department the need exists in, what activity is being performed where the need occurs, what the opportunity is for improvement, and what the relevant cost factors or benefits are. This should be set up as a quantifiable worksheet that enables you to estimate your total impact in terms of increased revenue, cost reduction, and/or cost avoidance.

Ideally, you have access to the customer's financial statements and are able to perform ratio analysis on them to identify where help is needed most. You can then show how your intervention can improve the company's financials. To do this effectively, you need to take the data in your cost-justification worksheet and develop a business case. You can access a sample cost-justification worksheet and business case from our online community at http://adriandavis.com/Free-Resources.

The business case should annualize all benefits and costs. For example, if you sell software on a per-user per-month basis, this needs to be converted to an annual number. The benefits that accrue must also be annualized. If there are any onetime costs (such as implementation), these costs should be spread over the life of the system. This enables an apples-to-apples comparison. The buyer can see that investing x per year with you will result in $(x + y)$ return per year. This is the logical justification needed to proceed. In addition to the return on investment, you can also calculate the payback period and the cost of delay. The buyer's total investment divided by the annual return will show how long they have to wait to get their money back. If your solution costs $100,000 and returns $200,000 per year, I know I will get my money back in 6 months. If your solution returns $200,000 per year, you can also calculate the cost of delay: $200,000 over 260 working days per year means the opportunity cost is approximately $800 per day. Every month we spend thinking of going forward is $16,000 of unrealized return.

It is this hard, objective logic that enables decisions to be approved within organizations with multiple decision makers. This logic silences the opposition. Two things are necessary for this financial analysis to be credible:

1. The numbers you use to calculate your impact on the organization can't be your numbers. They must come from the relevant managers within your buyer's organization, and these buyers must confirm them. Essentially you are always dealing with some unit and some frequency. Both the value of the unit and the frequency of the unit must come from the relevant manager. The number of errors, employees, customers, source documents, etc., must be their numbers. The value of salaries, benefits, costs, revenues, etc., must be their numbers. You are just bringing the data they gave you together in one place.

2. You must have a champion who emotionally wants your solution and who will use your cost justification as support for going forward. Your cost justification has no power by itself. It's just a financial analysis. Analysis doesn't move anyone. However, if you have successfully engaged someone emotionally, they will use your financial analysis to persuade others to their point of view.

Handling Objections Is Nonsense

If you want to be successful in sales today, *don't* handle objections. There are so many courses and articles focused on how to make you effective at handling objections. Some titles are: Handle Every Objection, Close Every Sale, Use Your Prospect's Objections against Them, etc.

Whenever you hear someone proposing to teach you how to handle objections, shut them down. They are hangovers from a past, dysfunctional era. Handling objections is an Industrial Age concept. It comes from a product-push philosophy. The corporation needed sales reps to sell its product. Prospective clients who would not buy were a problem. Sales experts then anticipated all of the potential reasons a prospective client might not buy and came up with approaches to address these objections. If the prospective client says they can't afford it, or if they say they need to check with someone else, use the Feel, Felt, Found Formula, which goes like this: "Really, Mr. or Ms. Prospect. I understand how you feel. Many of our clients felt the same way, until they found..." Successful sales reps came home with the order or the contract.

In today's postmodern world, handling objections is nonsense. Success today is not defined by how much you sell. Rather, success is defined by how well your solutions actually get implemented and the success you bring to your clients. Consequently, the quality of your sales matters more than the quantity. Of course, quantity matters. You have to make your targets. But you must make your targets by delivering real value.

Real value is delivered over time. Superficial value does not stand the test of time. If you do not deliver real value, your brand will suffer. In this age where everyone has a voice and everyone can amplify their voice, you can't afford to deliver superficial value. This means that you must partner with your prospective clients to ensure you can deliver value to them and to minimize the risk of delivery.

Rather than "handle objections," the focus of your sales effort in the latter stages of the sale must be on mitigating risk. Rather than wait for the prospective client to bring up reasons why they are apprehensive about proceeding and being forced into a reactive position, why not partner with your prospective client and proactively address this issue?

Risk Mitigation

Prior to signing the contract, schedule a meeting with your prospective client to address the issue of risk. You are in the business of helping your clients solve their problems. Remember, the issues you address are not your problems. They are your client's problems. This is an important realization. The burden is not on your shoulders; it's on your prospective client's shoulders. You are there to help them remove the burden. Home Depot had the right idea when their slogan used to be "You can do it. We can help." You are there to help, not to do everything. Sales professionals who don't realize this take on too much responsibility for the solution. Prospective clients knowingly or unknowingly collaborate with your sales rep to shift the burden of responsibility to your company. When things go wrong, you are to blame.

Your sales team should make it clear to the prospective client that your company is there to help. They should also make it clear that risk is involved. Based on their experience, they should proactively tell prospective clients the nature of the risks they believe the prospective client will face and solicit input, based on the prospective client's knowledge of their environment, of the risks they might face. Once all the risks are on the table, they should be grouped into categories based on severity and likelihood. Together, the sales rep and the prospective client should develop approaches to deal with the potential risks.

This approach keeps the responsibility where it belongs—with the prospective client. It also develops trust and respect. More than ever, prospective clients are looking for partners, not pitches. When you handle objections, you broadcast that you're only interested in making a sale. When you broadcast that you are only interested in making a sale, you trigger your prospective client's defense mechanism. When you help your prospective client mitigate risk, you broadcast very clearly that you are sincerely interested in building partnership. When you broadcast that you are interested in building a partnership, you inspire your prospective client to connect with you.

Conflict among Stakeholders

The future is coming fast! If your client's organization is like most, it is at risk. Changing client preferences, globalization, disintermediation, transmigration, and commoditization are just a few of the many forces acting on all industries. CEOs and other senior executives are doing their best to look out into the future, detect nascent threats and opportunities, and navigate their organizations safely through the turbulent waters. This is just what we'd expect from any good leader, and it's probably the fundamental motivation behind the executives engaging your firm.

So what's the problem? The problem is that navigating the turbulent waters involves change, and change always presents itself as risk for some. As I watch and assist leaders drive a change agenda, I often observe the conflict that emerges as a result. When people feel threatened, they go "reptilian." They shift into survival mode and often behave irrationally. Sometimes their actions can be dysfunctional. These dysfunctional behaviors can set off a chain of negative events similar to dominoes falling. Once the negative cycle begins, it can be hard to slow it down.

If we assume that everyone involved has good intentions, one way of understanding these conflicts is through Stanford University professor Philip Zimbardo's work on how time orientation dominates people's thinking.[1] People have one of three different time orientations: past, present, and future.

Leaders are typically visionaries, and as such they usually have a *future* orientation. All information that comes to them is filtered through the lens of the future. How will this affect strategy? How will this compromise or achieve my vision? Operational staff typically have a *present* orientation. They are all about getting work done efficiently. Information that comes to them is usually filtered through the question: how does this impact current work levels? Analysts typically have a *past*

1   Philip Zimbardo and John Boyd, *The Time Paradox: The New Psychology of Time That Will Change Your Life* (Free Press, 2009).

orientation. They are all about figuring out the root cause of problems. To do this, they consistently have to go back in time to understand why certain symptoms are presenting themselves. People who have a strong investment in the status quo also tend to have a past orientation. They like to look back on all the things they did to make the present what it is today.

Depending on which time zone you occupy, you will perceive change differently. A leader can present a wonderfully crafted initiative, only to be met with shock and horror by people who immediately understand the impact it will have on current workloads and by people who see it as a threat to everything they accomplished in the past.

The result?

Conflict. Followed by the erosion of trust.

Simply stepping back, assuming everyone wants what's best for the company, and understanding what a new initiative looks like from the different time orientations can be extremely constructive.

Proposing New Value from a Sales Perspective

From a sales perspective, when proposing new value I suggest the following:

1. Make sure you understand the impact of your proposal on the strategic objectives of the organization.

2. Don't assume because you have senior leadership support that your proposal will be accepted. Often the pushback from other parts of the organization will be strong and legitimate and sufficient to prevent your proposal from being acted on.

3. Take time to understand how your proposal builds on the good work done in the past. Is there a way to present your proposed change as a validation of the work that was done previously?

4. Get support from operations as to how the additional workload can be absorbed.

Once your proposed course of action is understood and supported from the perspective of multiple time orientations, it is much more likely to be implemented successfully.

CEO Action Plan

☐ Set up a role-play for your sales team to present a business case to you as a client.

☐ Help your team understand how their solution impacts the financial statements of their clients.

Sales Professional Action Plan

☐ Make a list of the risks your clients may face as a result of trying to implement your solution.

☐ Figure out how you impact the financial statements of your clients.

☐ Practice building a cost-justification worksheet.

Chapter 6

Phase Four: Action

Action expresses priorities.
—Mahatma Gandhi

O nce the engaged couple has considered all the pros and cons they decide that even though neither partner may be perfect objectively, they are indeed the right fit for each other. In this case the action is the official marriage ceremony: the wedding itself. They have now "tied the knot."

In the buying cycle, the action phase is quite similar: the proposal has been accepted and the risks have been evaluated and accepted. Both the buyer and salesperson agree that this is a right fit. The buyer is ready to sign the contract. Here's what the action phase looks like at a glance:

Buyer State of Mind: The buyer feels confident and wants to move forward.

Buyer Objectives: To get started and be clear on what happens next

Salesperson's Objectives: Ensure the buyer makes the commitment to change and is clear on what they need to do before you get started. Finalize terms and conditions.

Risks: Any lack of clarity around executing the contract or starting the project will cause delay or a return to the status quo.

The Close

This step in the buying cycle represented the climax in the traditional sales process. It was referred to as "the close," and often salespeople called this moment "smelling the kill." The psychology was completely rooted in product-push. Often, the harder the salesperson pushed, the harder the buyer would push back. If the buyer's will prevailed, the salesperson would feel resentment because of the amount of time he/she had invested. If the salesperson prevailed, the buyer would experience remorse at being forced into a decision they weren't ready to make.

I remember the first $1 million deal that I wrote. I was selling billing software and we were working out a partnership deal where our prospective client would embed our software in their solution. The projections were exciting. Our $1 million deal could easily grow to a $30 million deal. Not only was there huge upside, but we were negotiating the deal on the last day of our fiscal year. We really needed this deal.

Because it was such a high-stakes deal, and I had never negotiated a deal this size before, my director took over the negotiations. Our international VP of sales and our CEO also got involved via conference call. On the buyer's side, there was also a lot at stake. Given their financial projections, they needed to negotiate a deal that would optimize their profitability in the future.

What I learned as I sat back and watched was how not to negotiate. To say the negotiations were intense is an understatement. This was one of the most adversarial negotiations I have ever witnessed. We finally came to an agreement minutes before midnight. We got the $1 million deal and made our number for the fiscal year. However, in the process we lost the $30 million deal and the client relationship. When I called the COO the next morning, before I could finish my greeting he interrupted me and said, "Adrian, I never want to see your boss again!" When I hung up with him, I called my boss and told him what the COO said. His response? "Good! That means I'm doing my job!"

By "doing his job," what he meant was he was keeping the company's interests paramount. Making the number for the year was important for the stock price. That's what he saw as his job—extracting value from the client to create wealth for the shareholders. This is shortsighted. The true path to wealth is to meet the needs of our clients first.

Negotiation

The insights provided by Roger Fisher and William L. Ury in their book *Getting to Yes* (third edition, Penguin, 2011) are exceptional. They show how tough negotiations can actually enhance rather than erode or destroy relationships. *Getting to Yes* embodies true win-win thinking. The key principles from the book are:

- Separate the people from the problem
- Focus on interests, not positions
- Invent options for mutual gain
- Insist on using objective criteria

Focusing on interests instead of positions is key to leveraging buyer-pull and avoiding product-push. Interests are governed by goals, and as we learned earlier emotions are triggered for better or worse when goals are frustrated. The Getting to Yes process enables us to discover options that help our buyer get closer to their goals. This releases dopamine and causes them to feel good about their relationship with us. In the scenario I recounted earlier, my superiors got what they wanted so they felt great. My client felt that he got ripped off and felt stressed.

Since that experience, I had the opportunity to learn the Getting to Yes negotiation process and earned the confidence of my boss to negotiate multimillion-dollar deals singlehandedly. Today, I get a lot of pleasure passing these and other sales skills on to hundreds of sales professionals that enable them to enrich the lives of others while meeting and exceeding their own sales targets.

Getting over the Hump

The action stage in the buying process should be anticlimactic. Why? Because when we focus on buying rather than selling, we realize the purchase was made in phase 1. Buyers close gaps as soon as they realize they exist. When they proceed with the buying process, they do so with an answer in mind. Said another way, buyers purchase up front and then de-purchase as they discern their original choice was not the best.

Getting to the action step successfully means we must be far more concerned with how the buying cycle opens and less concerned with "the close." The gap was closed in the Awareness phase. That's where the energy to adopt change comes from. The formula we are concerned with is:

Remaining Motivation =

Awareness Energy - (Effort in Assessment + Anxiety in Apprehension)

If we didn't fill up in the Awareness phase, there will be insufficient motivation to proceed, sales cajoling notwithstanding.

The remaining motivation will not be as intense as the initial energy experienced in the Awareness phase. For this reason, it's important that you don't add unnecessary friction to doing business with you. Make it easy. Make your agreements clear and straightforward. Make the signing off process simple and unencumbered. Eliminate any potential confusion. Unnecessary friction can cause your buyer to delay and, as time passes, to potentially change his/her mind.

In addition to removing friction, it can also be effective to put an incentive in place. Rather than discount your service, is there some additional value-add (which doesn't require significant investment from you but would be highly valued by your client) you can throw in if the deal is executed by a certain date? Incentives like this appeal to the reptilian brain and create a sense of urgency to act and overcome the inhibitory response the cortex wants to impose.

CEO Action Plan

- ❏ Set up a role-play for your sales team to present a business case to you as a client.
- ❏ Help your team understand how their solution impacts the financial statements of their clients.

Sales Professional Action Plan

- ❏ Pick an upcoming negotiation and brainstorm what your buyer's real interests may be.
- ❏ Brainstorm what your interests are.
- ❏ Practice articulating why your interests are important.
- ❏ Find objective, third-party evidence you can use to evaluate the fairness of any deal that is reached.
- ❏ Practice role playing a positive negotiation. Let the sales team represent the buyer's interests and have the company executives represent the sales team.

Chapter 7

PHASE FIVE: ADOPTION

Those who cannot change their minds cannot change anything.
—**George Bernard Shaw**

T he wedding has taken place and the honeymoon is over. Now the real work begins as the couple starts their new life together. The marriage is far more than the wedding. Similarly, the adoption phase is a crucial phase of the buying cycle that occurs after the deal closes. Here's what it looks like at a glance:

Buyer State of Mind: The buyer feels fulfilled that they are meeting their objectives, or they feel resentment because their objectives are not being met.

Buyer Objective: To get to their desired future state as quickly as possible.

Salesperson's Objective: To ensure the buyer's expectations are exceeded.

Risks: Poor communication resulting in mismanaged expectations.

The Sale after the Sale

I can't say often enough how the world we are selling in today is so much more complex than the world of several decades ago, particularly with our continued tendency to focus on "the close" as the end of the sales process. Even the term "closed" implies something has been completed. From the seller's perspective it has, but the seller's perspective must be subordinate to the buyer's perspective.

From the buyer's perspective, all the effort the vendor has gone through to get the offer into the buyer's organization is invisible. This includes any effort from R&D, operations, logistics, and marketing, as well as sales. What the salesperson sees as "the close," the buyer sees as the opening act. In a very real sense, the jury is out and deliberating to render its verdict.

The probability of this verdict being positive for the vendor is low for the following reasons:

1. The salesperson's attention has shifted to new prospective clients.

2. Buyer environments are more complex technologically and politically.

3. The buyer may be governed more by avoidance goals than approach goals. Avoidance goals have a sneaky way of dominating one's thinking and causing buyers to sabotage themselves. Every racecar driver knows you steer into what you stare at. Staring at the wall because you want to avoid it is the fastest way to end up steering into it. When buyers crash, they don't usually blame themselves. It's much easier to blame the vendor.

4. Every purchase represents a desire for change. A desire for change and the implementation of change are two different things. Most change initiatives fail.

The Implementation of Change

Implementing change involves moving from the current state or status quo to a more desirable future state.

The status quo, while undesirable to the decision-maker, is often highly attractive to many in the organization. They perceive moving away from the status quo as undermining their value to the organization.

Attached to the status quo is a set of core beliefs. These beliefs are based on experiences and they drive a particular pattern of behaviors. This set pattern of behaviors perpetuates the same set of experiences, which in turn reinforces the belief system. It is a self-preserving cycle.

Forcing individuals out of their comfort zone triggers a reptilian response. While initially they may feel immobilized by fear, eventually they challenge the change from a place of deep-seated anger and resentment. More often than not, the leader who is driving the change effort is caught off guard by the intensity of the response and decides it's not worth fighting for. Those leaders who insist on moving forward, regardless of the initial response to the change, must still face the significant risk between the current and future states.

Between these two states lies the transition state. As I said earlier, the transition state is fragile. It is riddled with uncertainty, confusion, conflict, and disruption. And this uncertainty, confusion, conflict, and disruption is in the context of many other change initiatives taking place organizationally and in the personal lives of everyone involved. The combination of the attachment to current state and disruption of the transition state is often too much to overcome to get to the future state. Vendors would do well to ensure the approach goal of the future state is fully articulated and the risks of the current state are completely understood. They should also be prepared to serve in a coaching role to help the organization navigate change.

Making the sale is one thing. Making the sale after the sale is much harder and requires focused effort and attention.

Is Account Management Obsolete?

Many salespeople today go by the title account manager. What does this mean exactly? An *account* is defined as "an arrangement by which a body holds funds on behalf of a client or supplies goods or services to the client on credit."

As suppliers or salespeople, we have "accounts."

A *manager* is defined as "a person responsible for controlling or administering all or part of a company or similar organization." In today's complex business environment, clients don't want someone who thinks they are in "control" of their business, and they don't want a simple administrator. Buried in the title "account manager" is the Industrial Age concept that sellers are in control and client accounts must be managed. The Industrial Age has passed. Sellers are no longer in control, and buyers demand value from their interactions with sellers.

What's needed today is not account managers but client advocates. We need sales professionals who see a client as someone who has established a relationship with them to receive value over time. We also need sellers who recognize that they must collaborate with their clients. Whatever it is we are selling today, it must be customized in some way if it is going to have real value. That means the sales professional must understand the buyer's requirements (present and emerging) and represent those requirements back to his/her organization. This is advocacy. An advocate is "a person who publicly supports or recommends a particular cause." Rather than sellers who represent their own products and services, what we really need are consultative sales professionals who represent their clients while ensuring they are continually delivering sufficient value to their employers.

Let's change our language, our thinking, and our behavior and create a world where human beings collaborate, partner, and work together to create real value. We can't create symbiosis with Industrial Age assumptions.

The Problem with Twitter

Well, it's not just Twitter. It's Facebook, LinkedIn, and most of the new social networking tools. Twitter is probably just the worst offender. While the popularity of these social networking tools continues to skyrocket and our networks within them continue to expand, we have to ask ourselves if we are missing the point.

I am currently on Twitter, Facebook, and LinkedIn, among others. LinkedIn is my favorite, followed by Twitter and then Facebook. The danger I see with these technologies is that by their nature they are focused on quantity of connections rather than quality. In fact, services are now available where you can buy thousands of Twitter followers or Facebook friends. There is a built-in psychic reward associated with having a bigger network. Conversely, there is a personal, psychic penalty associated with having a small, fledgling network. The inevitable consequence is an inner hunger for ever more connections. But to what end?

Meaningful Connections

As humans, we are social beings. We need social connections. We thrive with healthy connections and wither without them. We also thrive with diversified connections. The person with a homogeneous group of friends, who all think and act alike, is likely to be narrow-minded and boring. Hanging out with people who have different perspectives challenges and broadens us. Learning different perspectives enables us to think with increasing layers of complexity and to think more creatively and intelligently.

Having lots of superficial connections does nothing meaningful for us or our connections. Social media is just a technology. It's just one of many ways we can reach out and touch others. It's flattering to receive emails notifying me that I have more followers on Twitter or to receive invitations to join different networks on LinkedIn or Facebook. Wouldn't you agree? However, as we reach out and make new connections, let's not forget to bring increasing value to the people who are already in our networks.

The younger generation is pushing the envelope in terms of how to make remarkable use of these technologies. However, when we rely exclusively on them, we miss the value of the rich interactions that come from actual contact. Every now and then it's worthwhile to pick up the phone or go to lunch and engage in the multifaceted communication that such media enable.

I recently took a look at my client list. Like you, I've got great clients! They're interesting and they're doing great things with their careers. I'm honored to have the opportunity to work with them. Spending time with people who know me and value my work and are open to a deeper relationship is far more valuable and rewarding than making another superficial contact. I think we consciously need to prioritize true and meaningful connections over superficial ones.

Please don't get me wrong. I don't have anything against social media. The danger is we can get sucked into chasing what we don't have rather than valuing what we do have. This is true personally as well as professionally. We need to look at the relationships we do have and realize how fortunate we are to have these people in our lives. We need to spend time thinking about how we can enrich their lives. Paradoxically, the more fulfillment we can create for the people who are already in our network, the more attractive we become to people who are outside our network.

I realize the younger generation is growing up with social media as a natural part of how they communicate, and they are able to communicate more effectively with text and Facebook messages. They might see picking up the phone or making a visit as inefficient. They want to be as efficient as possible. That's great; however, nothing beats actual face-to-face communication for effectiveness. There is something about being in the presence of another human being that communicates far beyond what is spoken. As much as possible, we need to find opportunities to spend time with those that matter to us.

In fact, Apple's successful retail chain is a great example of this. Apple made a huge investment in its retail outlets because it knew it had to be close to its customers. Steve Jobs understood something about face-to-face experiences. The Apple Store enjoys higher sales per square foot than any other retail organization.

Cameron Hay, former CEO of Unitron, who grew the company significantly in a six-year period, understood the power of face-to-face communication. He asked me to facilitate an event where he brought together his best customers and a cross-functional team of employees. Employees from sales, marketing, research and development, and other departments sat side-by-side with customers for an entire day as I facilitated a brainstorming session on the various ways Unitron could bring greater value to its customers. Unitron and its customers are still benefiting from the ideas generated and the relationships developed during that experience.

JoeAnne Hardy, CEO and Brett Bailey, Vice President of WBM Office Systems also asked me to facilitate a similar workshop. This was with one of their largest customers at the time. Again, a cross-functional team of employees spent the entire day with a cross-functional client team brainstorming ways to solve a specific challenge. Not only did they come away with exciting solutions, they also forged a deeper, more meaningful relationship with one of their best customers. JoeAnne and Brett also hold regular forums for the key executives in their target market to come together and discuss important issues affecting the industry.

When was the last time you created an opportunity for your customers and your employees to come together?

Front-End versus Back-End

I think the people who are spending an inordinate amount of time in social media are robbing themselves of rich relationships. Social media are just one of many lead-generation front ends to bring people into our network. But once they're in, then what? Investing in the back end is what matters. Build depth in your funnel so that as clients work with you, they are constantly amazed at the value you provide. Once you've got that figured out, social media, like other front-end technologies, will bring new people into your world and you'll be confident that their journey with you will be meaningful, fulfilling, and mutually rewarding.

Here are three things you can do to enrich your network and ensure you don't get caught in the superficial net of social media:

- Reach out to an inactive client and get caught up on what's happening in their world.
- Invite an active client to come to your office and talk about what's going on in their world and what their most pressing priorities and challenges are.
- Ask a longtime client to tell you what they value about you and how you might bring greater value to them.

Life is all about relationships. If we are not in meaningful relationships and doing meaningful work, we will be haunted by an increasing feeling of insignificance. Connections matter not because they are many, but because they are meaningful.

Account Strategy

What is the one glaring flaw that most salespeople have? It's their inability to formulate strategy. In fact, most salespeople have no idea how to develop an account strategy.

The game of chess has been around for centuries. Almost everyone knows how to play the game. However, there is a big difference between how an amateur plays chess and how a master plays. Fundamentally, that difference boils down to planning. An amateur plays tactically. They figure out what to do based on how the board looks at the time of their move. Masters formulate a plan, and each move takes them one step closer to the ultimate execution of that plan.

In sales, there is a strong emphasis on tactics (i.e., what to do and/or say once in front of a client). Most salespeople are adept at reading personalities and being persuasive.

Unfortunately, focusing on tactics forces them to decide at the time of each meeting what they should do next. Rarely will you find a salesperson who can show you an account strategy and explain how a single meeting fits into an overall plan.

To separate yourself from the masses of salespeople who call on your same accounts, begin to think strategically and formulate plans. A good account strategy should be written down and, at a minimum, comprise the following elements:

- Prospective client's business objectives
- Quantification of prospective client's needs
- Listing of key competitors with their strengths and weaknesses
- Listing of key influencers along with their disposition toward you and your competitors

- Listing of key decision criteria that will be used to evaluate your proposal
- An analysis of the quantifiable financial improvement as well as the intangible benefits your proposal will have on the organization
- A sequence of mutually beneficial steps/tactics required to move the account forward

Account strategy is a big subject, and by covering these seven areas you will separate yourself from the plethora of account managers who flit from meeting to meeting employing the latest sales tactic. Developing account strategy is the first step toward sales mastery. For more information on developing account strategy, visit the Human-to-Human Selling community at http://adriandavis.com/Free-Resources.

Implementing CRM to Support Your Account Strategy

First, I think we all believe there is something fundamentally sound about a company wanting to give its employees tools to do a better job of managing client relationships. When faced with the decision of whether to purchase a CRM solution, most reasonable executives will conclude that having a CRM solution is better than not having one. A decision is then made, and despite great hopes and promises, implementation is less than stellar. What can be done to avoid the high failure rates of CRM? Here are five tips:

1. Define a client relationship vision for your company. What are you moving toward? What will your company look like to an ideal client when he or she interacts with it? When there is a clear vision around the ultimate change that CRM will bring to your client's perception of your value, and it is clearly articulated and bought into, that vision will be realized despite the inevitable bumps in the road.

2. Have a clear roll-out plan. Don't try to boil the ocean. Figure out the key functionality you need implemented and set up a

timetable for when it will be rolled out. Take into account how your employees will respond to disruptive change. Give them time to adapt, and expect a temporary dip in productivity as they adapt to change. Select people who are respected by their peers but who are not technology geeks to lead your change effort. You want others to think, "Charlotte knows what she's talking about, and if she says this is good, it must be good. If she can do it, I can do it."

3. Ensure your CRM system can change easily. The mistake a lot of executives make in today's business environment is they see change as a revolution rather than an evolution. Most companies set up their systems as if they will not have to undergo another change for at least a decade. In today's business environment that can be fatal. Choose a system that can be easily adapted (ideally without any programming) as your market and internal requirements change. Get your employees to buy into the value of ongoing, evolutionary change. Feed them a steady diet of systematic, evolutionary improvement.

4. Analyze your client base and implement your CRM solution for your best clients. We recently did a client database analysis for a client and found that exactly 80 percent of their revenue came from exactly 20 percent of their clients. We also found that a very modest increase in sales from the top 20 percent of accounts would easily replace all the revenue from the bottom 20 percent. This is true for most companies. Invest in those clients who are willing to invest in you. Doing otherwise will stretch you too thin and dilute your value to those who matter. Many clients are not true clients. A true client wants and needs for you to be successful. Identify these clients, develop a more intimate relationship with them, and then adapt your company to meet their changing needs and definitions of value.

5. Be transparent. Choose a CRM solution that will allow you to share the information you are capturing on your clients with your clients. Most CRM solutions are closed. They were

designed with the mindset that since information is power, you should capture as much of it as possible and not share it. This will give you the "upper hand," the reasoning goes. In fact, all it creates is suspicion, and since your client truly has the power, that suspicion ultimately results in an adversarial, distant, and deteriorating relationship. Sharing information leads to trust and trust leads to a mutually beneficial, collaborative, and constructive relationship. You won't be able to have this relationship with all your clients. Nor do you want it. In the majority of cases, it doesn't matter what you do; these clients will never see you as anything more than a vendor to be commoditized. Having a proven model of mutually profitable and collaborative relationships will attract others in your client base to embrace this new way of working with you.

CRM is critical to success in today's market. However, your success will be determined by how you manage your relationships with the clients who value your company and see it in their best interests to work collaboratively with you. Information exchange and true client relationship management with these clients will yield tremendous financial, strategic, and psychic gains for you and your staff.

CEO Action Plan

- ❐ Help your sales team understand the risks associated with implementing your solutions.
- ❐ Develop ideas for risk mitigation that your sales team can use to collaborate with their clients.
- ❐ Define a CRM vision for your company. Get everyone excited about how you will use technology to look after your customers.

Sales Professional Action Plan

- ❐ Preplan exactly how you will reassure and onboard new clients.
- ❐ Lavish your customers with attention. Check in and see how they are doing emotionally.
- ❐ Analyze your client base. Ensure you are applying the appropriate attention to your right-fit clients.

PART TWO

REDEFINING CUSTOMER RELATIONSHIPS: FROM ADVERSARIAL TO HUMAN

Chapter 8

A BRIEF HISTORY OF CUSTOMER RELATIONSHIPS

History doesn't repeat itself, but sometimes it rhymes.
—**Mark Twain**

Whether we like it or not, the world is changing. Now that the Internet is a primary means of commerce and communication, our world has become more transparent, buyers have become more powerful, and businesses will have to change to compete in this new transparent environment.

Fortunately, the changes being forced upon us are good. They not only serve the best interest of buyers, they also serve the best interest of sellers.

You may be thinking, "Why do we need to change the way we do business? Haven't we spent a lot of time developing and delivering great products and services? Don't we deliver them on time? Haven't we brought down our costs to make our goods and services more affordable? Hasn't it all been done already?"

I understand. Those activities are more than enough to fill anyone's to-do list, and most salespeople are busier than ever. But those kinds of activities will only keep you busy; they won't make you successful in today's competitive marketplace. In fact, if you're comfortable with the status quo, you're not going to be in the marketplace in the very near future.

I'm not advocating simply doing more than what you're already doing. We've all heard the advice to work smarter, not harder. But what does that really mean? What practices do we have to change? The words of the philosopher George Santayana have never been truer: "To know your future, you must know your past." In order to know how to work smarter rather than harder in this new transparent business environment, we need to explore our past to understand our present and shape our future.

The Recurring Cycle of Change: A Historical Perspective

It seems to me that throughout history, a common recurring cycle of change occurs: first we begin with an *enlightened standard*, then a catalyst causes a period known (in retrospect) as the *Dark Ages*, a discovery results in a massive sharing of information to the masses known as a *renaissance*, and this causes a *reformation* that results in a visible cultural shift. Eventually this results in a new enlightened standard, which becomes the status quo—and the cycle begins again.

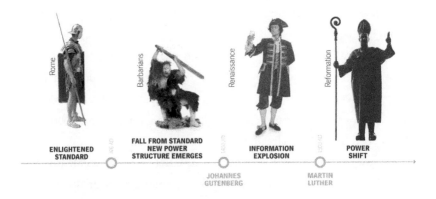

Figure 1.1. Cycling through the Ages of Change

The Enlightened Standard

For example, at one time the Roman Empire represented the enlightened standard and the status quo. Its influence spanned the known world with a degree of sophistication that had not been experienced to that time. However, because it grew too comfortable and eventually overextended itself, it collapsed in 476 AD.

The Dark Ages

After the Roman Empire's collapse, barbarians overran Europe. The barbarians were successful, not because of their great tactical measures or advanced weaponry, but because of the complacency of Roman society.

Had we been alive at this time, our primary concern would have been survival. It was an extremely dangerous time. The danger posed by the barbarians brought about a new power structure that led to the development of a multitude of kingdoms instead of the gigantic empire that had spanned most of the known world. These kings developed their own land-holding systems. They granted vast amounts of land to noblemen in exchange for their allegiance and taxes. These noblemen hired knights to protect their land and peasants to work the land.

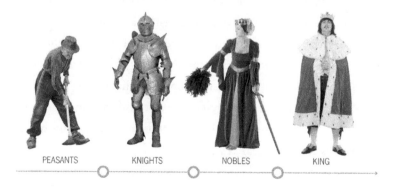

POWER STRUCTURE

PEASANTS   KNIGHTS   NOBLES   KING

Figure 1.2. From Kings to Peasants: The Power Structure

The peasants, at the bottom of the power structure, were relatively content because they were safe. (We should be able to relate to the willingness to give up freedom in exchange for safety given the risks associated with terrorism today.) Religion further reinforced their position with the notion that they should seek happiness in the afterlife rather than the present life.

This system, known as feudalism, brought safety and stability to society.

Renaissance

Then, in 1500 AD, Johannes Gutenberg invented the printing press. Prior to this, books were printed painstakingly by hand. Now books could be printed fairly quickly and inexpensively. This invention triggered the Age of the Renaissance: an age characterized by a renewed love for learning. Knowledge increased in every discipline (philosophy, psychology, music, art, mathematics, architecture, chemistry, biology, physics, and astronomy, to name a few), and this new knowledge was published in books. Europe was awash in books on every discipline.

Reformation

The very first book published on Gutenberg's press was the Holy Bible. Within fifty years of the Bible being published, Martin Luther, a lowly monk, led a successful revolt against the Catholic Church—the richest and most powerful institution on the planet at that time. This revolt led to the Protestant movement and the Age of Reformation. Martin Luther's protest was successful because he was able to gather support by telling his followers to read the Bible for themselves and see that some of the teachings of the priests were not biblical (e.g., the practice of indulgences, where people paid the priests to intervene on behalf of dead relatives who they feared were burning in hell).

The reason Martin Luther was successful was the relative ease with which people could access information. Information is power. When access to information shifts, power shifts with it. Consequently, renaissance and reformation will always go hand-in-hand.

The Enlightened Standard

The modern parallel to this historical cycle of change starts with the Age of the Artisan—the enlightened standard. Products were once handmade, and villagers had a real relationship with their suppliers. Each village had a butcher, a baker, and a candlestick maker. Tailors and shoemakers knew the hidden flaws of their clients and could customize their products to accommodate those idiosyncrasies. More importantly, they knew their clients and therefore could anticipate emerging needs before those needs were fully understood or articulated by their clients. For example, the shoemaker might proactively start working on a pair of shoes for the family whose first child is just about to begin walking.

The Dark Ages

This enlightened way of doing business, which was thousands of years old, collapsed in 1700 AD with the advent of the steam engine. James Watt's invention launched the Industrial Age (the Dark Ages of commerce). Huge factories were built with massive machinery that harnessed the power of steam. Artisans traded their customized craft for the safety of a regular paycheck. Mass production and mass marketing became the order of the day.

During this period, a new power structure emerged that was similar to the feudal system. The CEO was at the top, and underneath him was the vice president of manufacturing. Underneath the VP of manufacturing was the sales force, and below the sales force, at the bottom of the pyramid of power, was the customer. The customer was powerless. In fact, at this time the business literature did not refer to customers. It referred only to markets. Individual customers were not recognized, and they had no voice.

This powerlessness was amplified after two world wars. As people started putting their lives back together, there was a tremendous amount of pent-up demand. Anyone with the means to manufacture products found a ready marketplace. The formula for success was economy of scale. Produce more, lower your costs, and increase your profits. At this time business only cared about mass markets, mass marketing techniques, and gaining market share. Many of our dysfunctional sales processes were birthed in this industrial age.

Renaissance

In 1991, we had our Gutenberg moment. Sir Tim Berners-Lee invented the World Wide Web, and suddenly information could be published inexpensively. Remember, information is power. As noted earlier, when access to information shifts, power shifts with it. Consumers now have unprecedented access to information and, as a result, unprecedented power. Just as an individual successfully challenged the formidable power of the Catholic Church, today the youngest consumer can successfully challenge the formidable power of the largest corporations.

Reformation

Our current Age of Reformation can best be characterized with an illustration. Consider the case of Paul Christophero, president of PR firm Ocean Marketing, and Dave, a teenage customer who wrote him to inquire about shipment dates of a new product.[2] Christophero's firm represented a company that produced the Avenger Controller accessory for Sony PlayStation 3 (an innovative way for gamers, especially if they are disabled, to enjoy the PlayStation). The response to a polite customer inquiry quickly deteriorated as Christophero became cryptic, defensive, offensive, and impatient with young Dave. Dave then forwarded the very long email exchange to Mike Krahulik, who runs a major trade show and a website called Penny Arcade that has a very large following.

Krahulik tried to appeal to Christophero, but Christophero remained unbowed. Krahulik then published the exchange on his popular blog. Christophero, who had boasted about how powerful and well-connected he was, suddenly realized how powerful Krahulik was. The firestorm

---

2   If you would like to read the exchange unedited to grasp how far the communication deteriorated, you can find the exchange and the discussion it generated in its entirety on the Venture Beat blog: http://venturebeat.com/2011/12/27/ocean-marketing-how-to-self-destruct-your-company-with-just-a-few-measly-emails/. I apologize in advance for some of the language.

that followed forced the president of Avenger Controller to distance himself from Ocean Marketing and immediately fire Paul Christophero. When Christophero realized what he had come up against, he finally apologized. The exchange ultimately put him out of business.

This exchange, though unfortunate, is not isolated. Years ago, these exchanges between large corporations and seemingly insignificant customers would go unnoticed. Today, they end up going viral and force large corporations to climb down from their elevated perches.

Over the last two decades power has been shifting from the corporation to the client. But in the last few years, with the birth of social media, it's official: clients have now seized power and control.

This fact is evident in the vast universe of consumer-written product reviews and consumer blogs. The buying public now relies on those sources for information rather than the one-way sales pitches delivered by companies.

As in the Middle Ages, Renaissance and Reformation run together. When the production of information is democratized, the balance of power shifts. When the balance of power shifts, former abuses are no longer tolerated and the abusers suffer backlash if they don't reform.

Our Current Stage: The Modern Age of Reformation

Welcome to the Age of Business Reformation. Things have changed. The balance of power has shifted. We must now care about how we exchange with buyers. We must now operate with the understanding that buyers are in control of their exchanges with us.

Historically, sales efforts were perceived as the end of a long process that began with R&D (research and development); flowed through manufacturing, operations, and marketing; and eventually ended with the sales team transferring ownership of the product to the client. In this model, the sales team was perceived as the mouthpiece of the organization. Their job was to educate and tell the prospective client how great the company's products were. If objections surfaced, the salesperson's job was to "overcome" these objections and exert the company's will over the prospective client's.

I remember working for Encyclopedia Britannica as a teenager. I was trained in how to highlight the many excellent features of this great reference library. The main training, however, was on "handling" objections. We were trained to understand the different concerns potential customers would have and what to say as these concerns surfaced. Looking back, I realize I was being trained to ignore the customer's concerns and force the company's agenda. It was a battle of wills, and I was successful when the company's will prevailed.

This adversarial model no longer works.

Today, we must pay more attention to what constitutes a "right-fit client." Once we have identified this profile, we must be more willing to listen rather than talk. It is the vendor who needs to be educated, not just the prospective client. Today we are selling change. Change always involves risk. If risk is ignored in an age of transparency, both seller and buyer will get into trouble.

As client needs change, vendors run the risk of becoming irrelevant; conversely, they also have the opportunity to create new value.[3] Chief executives must employ the sales team as a source of strategic inputs. They must see the sales team as the ears of the organization, not just the mouthpiece. Those organizations that learn to listen and respond, as well as understand and accurately predict, will come out ahead.

Wayne Gretzky often explained his success on the ice by saying, "A good hockey player plays where the puck is. A great hockey player plays where the puck is going to be."

Today's business needs to go where the puck is going to be; they can get there by understanding historical patterns of change in general and becoming adept at uncovering the emerging priorities of their clients in particular. With respect to the latter, we will never get there if we can't first spend sufficient time with our clients.

---

3   \For more in-depth research on which sales strategies seem to be effective when salespeople are no longer a trusted source of information, see Brent Adamson, Matthew Dixon, and Nicholas Toman, "The End of Solution Sales," *Harvard Business Review*, July-August 2012, at http://hbr.org/2012/07/the-end-of-solution-sales/ar/1.

Chapter 9

SHIFTING YOUR FOCUS

You can't depend on your eyes when your imagination is out of focus.
—**Mark Twain**

Shifting Your Focus to Your Clients

I t's much easier to claim that you're client-focused than to actually demonstrate it in your day-to-day activities. In fact, most companies can't even identify what these behaviors look like, much less consistently demonstrate them. If you want a quick way to determine where you fall in the seller-focused versus client-focused continuum, look at what you pay attention to and in particular what you measure and reward.

Is your focus all about the numbers—sales volume, profitability, earnings, or share price? Or is it all about efficiency—production costs, price per widget, productivity, leanness? If the answer to either of these questions is yes, then you are probably seller-focused and not truly client-focused. I'm not suggesting that you stop paying attention to profitability and operational efficiency. Those are vital to maintaining your business. I am saying that those metrics are no longer enough and they are no longer primary. Such data is important—but only to you, not your client.

Operational efficiency is important, but clients don't care how efficient your operations are; they only care about the end result—how well it produces the outcomes they want.

Quality is obviously important, but not the quality of the production process. What's important is the quality of the end result. And only your client can define the perception of quality, not you.

Price matters to clients, but it's not price per se. It's value-for-money and cost to own or use that matter to your client.

Most of us have heard about the importance of "customer experience" to both our corporate strategy and our sales strategy. But many of us don't realize the difference between "customer experience" and "customer satisfaction." For example, if we ask customers to rate us on qualities that don't matter to them, we can show high customer satisfaction scores but still be completely ignorant about what our buyers truly value.[4]

In other words, if you continue to focus internally on production and profitability, you risk finding yourself doing a really good job producing something clients no longer want. You'll have put in place great systems for a product or service that is no longer desired.

Conversely, when you shift your focus to understand clients and involve them in the design, development, and marketing of your offerings, you'll be better positioned to meet current and future needs. When you proactively measure your ability to deliver what your clients desire, you'll be well on your way to becoming truly client-focused.

What does your client care about?

Research by Redline Advisors, a leading strategic executive advisory service, indicates that clients consistently look for four or five specific types of attributes in virtually all products, whether tangible or intangible:

---

4   For more about how to discern what your customers truly value and to put customer experience at the center of your strategy, see Forrester Research analysts Harley Manning and Kerry Bodine, *Outside In: The Power of Putting Customers at the Center of Your Business* (Amazon Publishing, 2012).

- Ease of use
- Timeliness
- Certainty (consistency, accuracy, reliability, predictability, safety)
- Cost to own/use
- Variety/choice

In spite of that research, companies rarely measure their product/service attributes from a client perspective. As a result, organizations are unable to proactively address client desires and expectations. As those wants and expectations evolve and change, data-focused firms risk losing more and more of their market share.

If we want to shift our focus to our clients, the first thing that needs to change is our understanding of value. We all want to sell "value-added" products. The problem is we don't know what value-added means. From an Industrial-Age perspective, it means we take raw materials and put them through a process that transforms them into a product. That process "added value." Today, this is no longer the case. It doesn't matter what we do if the customer is unwilling to buy what we are selling. Value is no longer under our control. Value is now a perception. It's like beauty. It's completely subjective and it's in the eye of the beholder. It is an internal experience.

The old value process looked like this:

Raw materials → Value-added process → Product

The new value process looks like this:

Idea → Desire → Valued resources → Action → Results → Reality

We are no longer in control of the creation of value. However, we can get better at discerning our buyers' perception of value through their behavior. The perception of value is demonstrated through sacrifice. When something is perceived as valuable, the buyer will sacrifice for it.

The buyer will give up their currency in exchange for the item of value because they perceive the item as more valuable than the currency they are giving up.

Money, however, is no longer the only currency the buyer trades for value. We must now recognize that today's buyer has two currencies: money and time. Of the two, time is more important. Money follows time. People invest time before they invest money. Yet, in a world of hyper-marketing, potential clients are bombarded with marketing messages. They tune us out. Getting someone to "pay" attention is becoming increasingly rare and increasingly valuable.

Salespeople of days gone by took the time they had with prospective clients for granted. Prospective clients were happy to meet with salespeople because back then salespeople were a source of information. This is no longer the case. Buyers feel there is very little a salesperson can "teach" them that they can't find out for themselves on the Internet. Buyers are no longer as willing to grant their time to salespeople.

However, today's salesperson needs to get time with the potential client in order to convert them to a paying client. Face-to-face time is one of the greatest predictors of sales success. A sales manager would do well to look at his sales staff's current calendar to forecast future sales. If the sales staff is successful in booking time with senior executives today, odds are they will have good sales three to six months from now (or the appropriate time lag for the specific industry).

Time with buyers is a leading indicator. Money is a lagging indicator. This is why sales teams need to view time as the more important of the two currencies. Those prospective clients that are willing to "spend" time with you will eventually spend money. Time and attention are the newly coveted metrics in the Age of Reformation because they indicate what the buyer truly values.

In most companies, rewards are focused on production and volume. The more widgets you make at a cheaper price, the better. The more people you call on and the more widgets you sell, the better. Again, there's nothing inherently wrong with this approach or these kinds of measures. It's simply that business has moved on, and this type of measurement breeds and rewards behaviors that are no longer valued by clients.

It is unrealistic to expect organizations to change dramatically overnight. However, companies that don't begin to shift their focus place themselves at risk of quickly losing clients. People tend not to buy from firms that fail to solve their problems or meet their wants.

As in the Middle Ages, the Age of Reformation is inexorable. In fact, the powerful nations of the United Kingdom, the United States, Canada, and so forth, are the outgrowth of the Reformation. These nations have produced unprecedented wealth, the likes of which the world had never seen before. Resistance to the Reformation in the Middle Ages was futile. Resistance to reformation today is futile. It's happening. The ground beneath us is shifting. Decades and centuries from now, historians will look back and say our age was an age of significant transition. Rather than resist the business reformation, companies should embrace it!

Down with Client Dictatorships!

However, many company executives, understanding the implications of losing clients, simplify the matter for their employees by adopting the policy that the client is always right. But in some cases this policy has gone too far. Many buyers now habitually abuse their suppliers. We've gone from large corporations abusing clients to clients abusing even the largest of corporations.

Consumers are no longer satisfied with just receiving mass merchandise. Access to instant information and greater choice has enabled buyers to wield unprecedented power like that of a king or dictator. The pendulum has swung from corporate to client dictatorships.

Again, the adversarial model doesn't work in the long term. It's not sustainable. The modern client has to realize that along with expanded rights and privileges comes responsibility. The pendulum has swung too far and needs to swing back to a balanced position. In fact, we've entered a time of correction in which companies are waking up to the detrimental impact of non-profitable clients and are beginning to fire these clients.

What we need is a mutual meritocracy where both sides realize we need each other and we must begin to treat each other with mutual respect. Both sides need to earn our way into a richer relationship. In a meritocracy, leaders are chosen not by their birthright or their wealth but by their value. In other words, our business relationships need to become *symbiotic.*

Human-to-Human Selling: The Strategy of Symbiosis

Symbiosis simply means "life together"—with the implication that the results are greater than the sum of their parts. When two complementary living organisms combine and symbiosis results, a new reality is created that wasn't possible before.

Besides being a powerful natural phenomenon in its own right, symbiosis has also been a powerful metaphor for a number of different concepts. Symbiosis is the secret behind the magic of cooking, and it is the foundation of marriages that retain their spark decades after the couple says "I do." It is also the key to success in sales.

The truth is that companies and clients need each other. One has what the other lacks: the client needs the company's expertise, and the company needs access to the client's world to better understand what is valued and what will be valued, and eventually the client's money to be able to keep delivering that value. In the case of the right-fit client, the resulting profitable partnership truly is greater than the sum of its parts. Recognizing the symbiotic potential in business relationships is truly the difference between thriving and surviving (or going out of business).

Although the practical difference is profound, shifting to a symbiotic approach in selling, as opposed to an adversarial one, doesn't take a lot of work. In fact, if you've ever been in a long-term relationship, you already know how to do it. It's a simple mindset shift that largely comes from letting go of what we think we know about sales (such as the common notion that companies and customers are opponents) and recognizing and following what happens naturally in relationships and potential partnerships.

Whenever we do our sales training workshops, the part of the training that impacts participants the most is our discussion about the foundational role of emotion in the sales process. Emotion drives everything! Most managers track sales success by short-term or limited-term quotas—and quarterly quotas, for instance, don't reflect the real time investment and skills it takes to build a long-term, mutual, symbiotic customer relationship. Relationships take time and skills—and the real asset is the customer relationship, not the short-term sale.[5]

The problem is that most salespeople have been trained in an adversarial approach that precludes the possibility of symbiotic relationship building. Such an approach turns every sales potential into a zero-sum game, where the best you can hope for is an equitable truce. When companies and customers are fundamentally on opposing sides, every negotiation is a fight, and every time one side gains the other side loses. Even when the deal is inked and both parties shake hands, they emerge feeling battle-worn and they are loath to develop trust.

Imagine this dynamic in a marriage relationship—or any relationship, for that matter. When spouses feel as if they are fundamentally on opposing sides, they also feel as if they have to fight to get their due in every interaction. Put simply, the spouses would be enemies, not lovers. Trust is absent. Symbiosis is impossible.

Now, this isn't a book about marriage, but it's enough to say that lasting marriages evolve beyond the battle of the sexes. Differences don't have to divide, and if one side has something the other needs, that can be cause for a mutually supportive and dependent relationship that releases energy rather than drains it. Marriage, at its best, is a symbiotic relationship where the result is greater than the sum of the complementary parts.

Just think about how the quality of life for both spouses would increase if every interaction produced energy and affection rather than drained them. You'd wake up each morning viewing life as an adventure.

---

5   For more about how customers are the true assets of a company and how to measure their value, see Don Peppers and Martha Rogers, *Return on Customer* (Crown Business, 2005).

You'd be able to support each other's unique gifts and interests, because your spouse's success would feed your success, and vice versa. With a relationship built on the foundation of trust, you'd be freer to take risks and pursue your dreams. And, yes, there'd be a lot more of that literally symbiotic act that creates children too.

The same can be true for the relationship between company and client—and the sales team can be the catalyst. We hope there's no literal symbiosis, of course, but creative ideas, strategies, and even entirely new business endeavors and joint ventures can emerge from a symbiotic business relationship.

Based on my own experience in sales and sales training, the people who love sales are also the kind of people who love people. The truly great salespeople love helping people and creatively coming up with solutions that generate win-win situations for their company and their customers. If that doesn't describe the essence of symbiosis, I don't know what does.

Quite frankly, symbiotic, human-to-human selling works because it honors the way relationships naturally develop. But H2H selling is more than just a technique to land the sale and build value for the company. It's also a strategy in which the sales force can serve as a catalyst for not only symbiosis with individual customers, but enterprise-wide symbiosis from the ground up.

Most business books on customer-centricity and change management are aimed toward the C-suite, assuming that strategic change must begin from the top down. But what if the more effective and natural approach to making the enterprise customer-centric (i.e., symbiotic, or positioned to serve the customer in a mutually profitable way) is to begin from the outside in—with the sales force, where the customer relationship begins? If the sales force can internalize and practice the symbiotic sales approach in their customer relationships, they can also be the catalyst to jumpstart the client-focused chain reaction for the entire enterprise.

In the following pages, I'm going to share with you a sales strategy for creating symbiotic business relationships no matter what field you're in. If you embrace the changes outlined in this book, your business and your sales funnels will be more robust. Whatever level of sales deals you are focused on now, you will be able to easily double or triple the size of your deals. You will be able to align your company with better-suited clients. And you will feel more confident as you navigate the incessant and sometimes abrupt winds of change by patterning your sales strategy after one of the most basic energy-releasing dynamics in nature: mutual dependence. Symbiosis.

Crafting Your Sales Strategy

Increasingly, sales leaders are being scrutinized for their ability to lead strategically.

What is strategy? Strategy is the effective use of limited resources to achieve a desirable end.

Your corporation has a strategy, which includes its mission, values and vision. Your sales strategy must advance the corporate strategy. Your vision must move your company closer to its vision. Your strategy is really a strategic initiative, which propels your company toward the fulfillment of its corporate strategy.

Step 1: Define the Business Results

The first step is to understand the business results you are on the hook for. In the next 3-5 years, does your company need to double or triple in size? Is there a target with respect to market share? Customer satisfaction? Something else? These goals are often non-negotiable as the company hired you to achieve these results. You either achieve them or they will find someone else to achieve them.

Step 2: Gather Information

The next step is to do an assessment. Most sales leaders go from year to year without ever stopping to assess the health of their organization. Can you imagine what would happen to your personal health if you never visited a doctor for a check up? How many serious ailments would go undetected until it's too late? Your organization is no different. Develop the discipline to perform an annual check up before your craft your strategy. This is especially important if you are in the process of transforming our organization from a product-centric organization to a client-centric one.

A SWOT analysis, which is a structured way of looking at your company's strengths, weaknesses, opportunities or threats, is helpful here. Strengths and weaknesses are internally oriented. Anything within your organization that helps you achieve your goals is a strength. Anything that inhibits your goal achievement is a weakness. Opportunities and threats are externally focused. Anything in your environment that can help you achieve your goals is an opportunity; anything in your environment that inhibits your goal achievement is a threat.

For the internal assessment of sales organizations, we use a sales audit checklist. We've been able to show our clients many surprising insights as a result of going through this process. The audit should identify what is giving your company its current momentum and enable you to make informed decisions for leveraging your strengths and minimizing your weaknesses. Your internal check up should be treated formally and comprise the following:

a. A comprehensive checklist that forces an objective examination of your marketing, sales, delivery, customer support and sales support services and their ability to create value for your prospective clients and customers. You should look at the inputs and outputs of all your processes and identify obstacles to sales productivity and hindrances to customer delight. Use this examination to uncover how well your sales team understands your vision, mission and values and how well their compensation drives the desired behaviors. Look at your reports and how well they are communicating the right information to the right people at the right time.

b. Qualitative interviews with your sales team and sales support staff to understand what is working and what is not working from their perspective. Develop a "hassles" list and prioritize these hassles based on how much they interfere with sales productivity and customer delight.

c. A "current state" process map. This map is based on the 1:1 interviews done with the sales team as well as one or more group workshops. A cross-functional team should be put together that best represents how you sell. An experienced facilitator can then draw out from the team what they do on a day-to-day basis and convert their descriptions into a flow chart. A word of caution: it's important to have people who actually understand the sales process facilitate these meetings. Salespeople have little patience educating people who don't understand sales, but they love to talk openly with people who "get it" and can quickly grasp their observations and drill down on them. Sales teams are invariably surprised when they see what they do accurately represented in a process map. Identified hassles should also be represented on the map so everyone can clearly see the opportunities for improvement.

In addition to the sales audit, interviews with customers are a key component of your environmental scan. Ideally, have an independent third party perform these interviews and target the most senior decision-makers in your client organizations.

When we do these interviews for clients, we use them as opportunities to understand the value our clients are delivering to their customers, the value their customers are expecting and what their customers' observations are of the industry and our client's company. It's amazing what can be uncovered in a well-orchestrated telephone conversation with senior executives. We use these conversations as opportunities to uncover our client's customers' strategic objectives. What are these customers aiming to accomplish over the next three years? What is most pressing for them this year?

This information should be collected with no expectation that it relate directly to the products or services you provide. You want to aggregate this information to get an understanding of what your clients are trying to accomplish. As you aggregate this information, you will gain great insights into how you can deliver greater value to these customers. Remember, your value is all about how you help other people achieve what they are trying to achieve. The strategic objectives that your skilled interviewer uncovers in these discussions represent the collective desire of your client's organization. We'll discuss this more when we discuss the Awareness Phase in the Buying Cycle.

A competitive analysis should also be part of your environmental review. Be careful not to define your competition too narrowly. According to Michael Porter, a leading authority on competitive strategy, your competition is any force that can reduce your company's profitability. These include direct rivals, new entrants, substitutes, suppliers and even some customers.

Step 3: Set Your Sales Objectives

Once the check up is complete, use the insights as inputs to setting your strategic objectives.

Define clearly what your sales team must accomplish in the next one to three years in order for you to deliver the business results expected of you.

You can't do everything and you can't be everywhere. Based on your findings, what are the specific areas in which you need to invest? Do you need to improve your lead generation? What about your recruiting, hiring or on-boarding processes? Your funnel management? Your client engagement? What structural changes will need to be made? What does your team need to look like in order to have effective market coverage? How do you need clients, prospective clients, competitors and suppliers to perceive you?

Decide on what will make the biggest impact in enabling you to achieve your business results.

Step 4: Set Your Metrics

You need to steer your sales ship and, when necessary, make course corrections. The only way you can do this proactively is if you have the right metrics. We like to share the following formula with our clients:

$$Y = f(x)$$

It says that Y is a dependent variable and it depends on "x", which is an independent variable. In other words, we have no direct control over the variable Y. Instead, we can influence it, by changing "x".

To relate this to sales, you have no control over whether or not you will achieve your sales number. You can influence your achievement of this number, however, by directing the behavior of your sales team. The behaviors of your team are what you can control and the metrics you watch need to be related to these behaviors. For example, the number of leads they generate, they number of meetings they have, their level of preparation for these meetings, the level of insight they have to share with their prospective clients, the number of proposals they generate, the quality of these proposals and the quality of their sales funnel are all examples of activities that have a direct influence on your ability to achieve your sales numbers. Having metrics around how well and how often these activities occur is of far more value to you as a sales leader than monitoring sales numbers. Managing a sales team based on sales numbers alone is like driving by looking through the rear view mirror. Trying to correct course based on where you've been is completely ineffective. You want to steer based on what's ahead not what's behind.

Step 5: Determine Actions

You now have the clarity to determine what specifically needs to get done. Break your sales objectives down into specific steps that need to be completed with start and end dates and assign them to specific people. Make this a focus for each quarter. Don't try to achieve everything at once. Each quarter, draw up a list of specific actions that need to be focused on and get your team's agreement that if it goes on the focus list for the quarter, it gets done no matter what.

Step 6: Create a Contingency Plan

There's a saying in the military that says something like, "No plan survives contact with the enemy." That is a critical insight. Planning is important, but flexibility is also important. Try to anticipate what might go wrong and how you will react. What if your competition responds in a pronounced way? What if a key employee leaves? What if your sales number is increased? What if the economy falters?

Try to think of likely scenarios and how you'll respond to them. That way you will not freeze from shock when your assumptions are challenged.

Step 7: Get Results and Repeat the Process

With a plan behind you, you can now act with definiteness of purpose. Keep your people focused.

At the end of the year, repeat the process. Review the findings of your last audit and identify any outstanding or emerging issues. Review and revise your Critical Success Factors. Update your tactical plans and plan for training and coaching your team to success.

Coaching for Success

Don't forget to coach your people in order to get them to deliver the results you're looking for.

Every salesperson needs a coach. Be careful, however, how you distribute your attention or the attention of an outside coach. Most sales leaders engage only in remedial coaching (i.e., someone goes on a 90 day performance improvement plan and they're given coaching to help them save their job.). Don't make this mistake. To achieve superior results, ensure your best reps get a disproportionate amount of your attention or the attention of an external coach. Let your team know that coaching is a privilege.

Also, ensure you are coaching with purpose. Coach your team to the behaviors they were trained on. Identify the key behaviors that must become habits for your organization to perform at the next level. Have them record how they are performing and ideally, expose the execution of the new behaviors the whole team so that members can see how well they are engaging in these required behaviors compared to the rest of the team. This keeps your team focused on performing specific actions. These new actions, once habituated, are what will drive new results for you. Keeping the team focused on the execution of these actions is what will ensure your strategy gets executed.

As a sales coach and mentor, if you want to see peak sales performance, you must be proactively involved in the development of each of your people and provide on-going feedback and follow-up. Coaching is a process equipping people with the tools, knowledge and opportunities they need to become more effective.

Coaches don't actually develop people. They equip people with what they need to develop themselves. Rarely will you have the time to involve yourself with every aspect of someone's development. And rarely, will you possess all the information, skills and wisdom that someone might need to ensure their development.

Be A Catalyst

Fortunately, there is no need to be perfect to be an effective coach. Instead, view your role as a catalyst for development. As a coach, you will advise, instruct, facilitate and appraise. Advising means communicating expectations and sharing information. Instructing means clarifying and teaching. Facilitating means assisting with the change process. Appraising means providing on-going feedback.

Don't Make Excuses

Coaching often breaks down because leaders are not committed to it. They often feel uncomfortable with this personal level of contact. Consequently, they will hide behind excuses such as:

- I'm too busy,
- I don't know all the answers,
- I'm not a psychologist,
- I have more important responsibilities,

- If there are no promotions available, what's there to talk about?
- My subordinate is not open to feedback.

None of these excuses are valid. If you are committed to your vision, you must coach and mentor your people.

Successful Coaching

Successful coaching occurs when:

- Employees know where they stand
- They commit to what's expected
- They know they are valued
- They feel challenged and supported
- They know where they are going
- They are given feedback on their progress

Five Step Process

Here's a practical 5-step process for successful coaching:

1. Agree on the topic. What is the specific purpose of this coaching?
2. Set a specific contract. What is the outcome we are aiming for? Make your support for their development clear.
3. Provide feedback.
4. Praise and reinforce.
5. Provide closure.

As the coach, keep a log of your interactions with your people. Make a note of the current situation with one of your employees where coaching is required with a simple statement such as, "the coaching objective is to help _____ get better at _____."

10 Tips for Successful Coaching

1. Request our free Coaching Log to log your coaching interaction with your employee as you follow the 5-step process. You'll find

it in the free resources section at http://adriandavis.com/Free-Resources. Record the date, the major outcomes of the session and any insights gained in the process.

2. Set a specific contract of the things that you will do and the things you expect them to do.

3. Record the specific feedback that you provided, how that feedback was received, and the date of each interaction.

4. As progress is achieved, record the specific progress and praise your employee for their development.

5. Record in your log how you acknowledged the progress.

6. When the new behavior is finally achieved, acknowledge the achievement and bring the coaching around to closure.

7. When you give feedback, try to be specific. Avoid vague generalizations. Also, aim to be descriptive. Without being judgmental, describe the behavior that you are observing, focus on the behavior rather than the person.

8. Always try to be respectful and avoid a sense of superiority. Demonstrate real concern and understanding.

9. Be sure to be timely with your feedback by giving it as soon as the behavior occurs.

10. Finally, as a coach, ensure that your feedback is actionable. Make sure that your subordinate can actually do something with the feedback you are providing.

Please let me know if you have other ideas on how to coach your sales team successfully, and feel free to download the coaching log at http://adriandavis.com/Free-Resources.

In the next chapter, we'll discuss redefining the roles of the buyer and seller, the five levels of customer relationship, and why defining your right-fit client is so crucial to creating symbiosis.

Chapter 10

Selling to Humans:
The Five Stages of
Relationship Development

*The meeting of two personalities is like the contact of two chemical
substances: if there is any reaction, both are transformed.*
—Carl Jung

I n the Dark Ages, scientists held a geocentric view. They believed
the earth was fixed and that it was the center of the universe.
Copernicus, with his naked eye, perceived that the earth was in
orbit around the sun. Galileo later confirmed his findings. Both men
met with fierce opposition when they published their findings, because
when the center of the universe changes, everything changes.

To draw the modern parallel, during the Industrial Age clients existed
for the firm and the firm's products were the center of the universe.
The product attracted prospective clients. Salespeople were filled with
product knowledge so they could wax eloquently on the virtues of the
product. The "build it and they will come" philosophy reigned supreme.
Businesses expanded and/or increased profits by driving the unit costs
down through economies of scale.

The sales force was the mouthpiece providing information about the product and writing orders. This was the time of filling warehouses of unsuspecting clients with product in exchange for volume discounts. The sales staff or management thought little of the long-term relationship with the company and the client.

Industrial Age salespeople were busy with the "product-push" method of selling and did little or no information gathering. They would have been hard pressed to guess what a client's needs might be six months down the road. Their Rolodex was confined to the personal information of their contact; it contained a reminder about birthdays and anniversaries so that the appropriate card would be mailed three days in advance. Even today, despite the explosion of customer relationship management (CRM) software, many companies have done little more than automate their salespeople's Rolodexes. (As we'll discuss in Part 3, CRM should be a company philosophy, not just a technology.)

But in the Age of Business Reformation, where the purpose of business is to create value for clients, businesses must know who they are in business to serve. To avoid client dictatorships and achieve symbiosis, the business cannot get trapped in the gravitational pull of any client that gets too close. The symbiotic business cycle demands the definition of the *right-fit client*. The business must hold the right-fit client as the center of its system. The right-fit client is like the sun that radiates energy and enables the company to have life.

Just as in the Middle Ages, as we shift from a world where the company placed itself in the center of the universe to a world with right-fit clients at the center, many will be unhappy. Changing the center of the business universe changes everything. Traditional practices will be seen as ineffective at best and potentially harmful.

Redefining the Sales-Client Relationship

With this new center of gravity, successful business transformation depends on deep and strategic client relationships. And the sales force is critical to the development and nurturing of these relationships. Not only do we need to refocus our attention on the client and put them at the very center of our universe, we must also become strategic enablers helping clients achieve their objectives and grow their business.

It is no longer enough to be a good supplier or even a desired supplier. The efficiencies and means of "supplying" that helped us achieve this status no longer offer any competitive advantage. We must supply more than a good product or service for the client's use today, because today quickly becomes yesterday. Client needs change, and with those changes their perception of our value also changes. And if we're not careful, we can quickly become redundant.

True competitive advantage lies in our ability to create symbiosis with our right-fit clients. This means that we must become not just *trusted advisors* but *symbiotic partners*. This is how we are able to have the biggest impact on our client's success. While trusted advisers are valuable, at the end of the day they are still suppliers. In order to achieve a strategic connection, we must successfully link our value to the client's strategies and priorities—which means we must be knowledgeable about their world, their challenges, their strategies, and their decision criteria.

Further, the art of knowing our clients must be continuous and dynamic so that we not only meet their needs today but also anticipate their future needs. We will then be in a position to partner with our clients on a long-term basis to help them succeed and grow. In short, we must not only put our clients at the center of the universe, we must also be orbiting right there with them.

From Stranger to Symbiotic Partner: The Five Stages of Client Relationships

Just as history goes through recurring cycles, client relationships also go through a cycle. Relationships with clients should evolve over time for your firm to succeed in this new dynamic economy, and they seem to move through five distinct stages. Being familiar with these stages helps the participants move through them more quickly, as they can more readily satisfy the buyer's requirements for each stage. It is equally important that a client relationship goes through every stage. Knowledge provides the map for growth.

From your perspective, client relationships begin with suspects and prospective clients. From the client's perspective, the relationship begins with you as a *stranger* pursuing them (stage one). When your sales team successfully converts a prospective client into a client, from the client's perspective they are the ones who have done the converting. They have converted your company from a stranger to a *supplier* (stage two).

With the consistent and dependable delivery of value over time, you will eventually be converted into a *desired supplier* (stage three). The adjective "desired" connotes emotion. Great service and true value are hard to find. At this stage, the relationship changes from a transactional one to an emotional one. When a client experiences it, they can't help but become emotionally engaged with your company. Trust goes way up and doors swing wide open. It is at this stage that you must engage in strategic account management if the relationship is to advance.

Remember desire is like the fax machine ringing. Something in the invisible realm is about to get replicated in the visible realm. When you're desired as a supplier, it's because you are perceived as an important part of this process.

By demonstrating you can provide more than a good product or service and by offering insights that help the client achieve their objectives, you put yourself in position to become a *trusted advisor* (stage four).[6] By expanding the partnership to a business-to-business strategic collaboration, you position your company to achieve the ultimate relationship status—*symbiotic partner* (stage five).

Note: These stages reflect how the client sees you, which sometimes differs from how you see yourself. In order to get full value from this and other guidance in this book, begin with a realistic understanding of where you are today and what it takes to move to a higher level. After reading this section, if you'd like to assess your client relationships objectively go to http://adriandavis.com/Free-Resources and access the Symbiotic Relationship Assessment.

---

6   Trusted advisor is certainly a common term now, but many of us were introduced to the term by David Maister, Charles H. Green, and Robert M. Galford in their book *The Trusted Advisor* (Simon & Schuster, 2000).

RELATIONSHIP LIFECYCLE

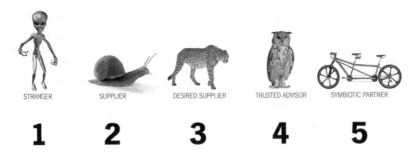

Figure 2.1. From Stranger to Symbiotic Partner.

Let's take a closer look at the five stages.

Stage One: Stranger

The first level of relationship is essentially no relationship. You are a *stranger*. The client isn't aware of you or your business and/or doesn't see a reason to learn more about you or do business with you.

You are on the outside looking in. And, more likely than not, the thought of doing business with you creates some level of anxiety for the target client, which means you've got some major hurdles to jump to make it to the next level. It also means you need to rethink your marketing and lead-generation activities. Instead of chasing prospective clients, what can you do to attract them and increase their trust and comfort level with you? How can you reward them for paying attention to you?

Stage Two: Supplier

At stage two, you have won the business. Your new client decides to buy from you and considers you a *supplier*. They trust you to deliver a product/service that meets their needs, but the relationship is transactional in nature. The relationship was "sealed" based on the sales professional as an individual, but it continues based on price and utility.

At this stage of the relationship, there is not enough familiarity or trust to assume repeat business or to move the relationship from one of transactions to something deeper.

Typically, the response or focus of the supplier is "pushing" the value proposition, marketing message, or the benefits of what is offered to educate the client so that the next transaction can be secured and the relationship can grow.

Stage Three: Desired Supplier

At stage three, your client begins to become emotionally engaged in the relationship. You have successfully shown them that you will not only meet their expectations, you'll exceed them in ways that are important to them. Consequently, they are interested in other products or services you provide and seek to give you a greater share of their wallet and/or enter into a longer-term relationship.

The client feels they can now depend on you for attention and support. In much the same way as they view you as a *desired supplier*, they expect a similar approach and treatment in return. They want to be treated as a desired and special client.

The client's fundamental assumption at this point is that the future relationship is secure if you continue to pay attention to their needs. In this case, that means the product/service will continue to perform the way it has in the past, and that the quality will meet or exceed previous standards. Consistency is an important aspect of the desired supplier relationship, as are quality, price, and reliability.

Even as a *desired supplier*, price continues to be an important aspect of the relationship. However, it is not as dominant a factor as the pure *supplier* relationship because it is presumed that you have committed to a longer-term relationship and consequently, your prices are fair. This commitment allows you to invest in processes that ensure functional efficiency, which reduces costs in operations, sales, and marketing.

Stage Four: Trusted Advisor

At stage four, the game changes dramatically. You are no longer judged merely on price and utility. You have demonstrated your ability to offer meaningful ideas and insight. You have shown yourself as a valued member of the team. The client views you as a *trusted advisor*. They turn to you for advice and offer advice on how you can increase your value to them.

To be able to view you as a trusted advisor, the client must trust first that you understand them on a person-to-person level and, secondly, that you can provide insight that is strategically relevant to them. This level of engagement is possible because the client is receptive to input and insight from you. And that is possible because of your proven effectiveness in providing that input and insight. You not only have demonstrated that you provide consistent value and "know" their business, but you have also positioned yourself to participate in a way that is meaningful to the client. In the hundreds of interviews we've done with executives, one of the consistent themes is that this level of trust must be earned. It takes time. You must demonstrate that you really have their best interests at heart. If you can't perform well as a desired supplier, it is unlikely that you'll be invited to perform as a trusted advisor.

That being said, it is very difficult for sales professionals to provide a relevant and meaningful level of interaction if they have not experienced that type of engagement in their own company. If salespeople are not conscious of corporate strategy as it relates to their own business, it will be difficult for them to speak from a place of authenticity when speaking to prospective clients about strategic issues. In short, salespeople must become engaged in their own organization at a strategic level for them to operate the same way with a client. They must be able to come to the table as a peer—as a business executive rather than a salesperson.

For some executives, this is very scary. They want to keep their strategies private. They want a sales force that just sells, sells, sells! Why distract them with important things like strategy? There are several things wrong with this approach:

1. First, it assumes salespeople are not capable of understanding strategic issues and that time spent educating salespeople should be spent educating them on product knowledge. The negative consequence of this approach is twofold. The firm will tend to hire people who are capable of rehearsing product facts and figures rather than people who have the intellectual muscle to think big-picture. The other consequence is that the firm's salespeople will talk in product language. The way they speak determines who they will be able to speak to. People who speak strategically are often invited to speak with people who speak strategically. People who talk in a transactional manner tend to be invited to speak with people who also speak in a transactional manner.

2. In my experience, executives who want to keep their strategy private need to be the smartest people in the room. Fundamentally, they are insecure. This deep-seated insecurity permeates the culture of the organization. Fear and bureaucracy frame the culture. In a complex and fast-changing environment, leaders need to surround themselves with entrepreneurial and creative thinkers. Lack of sharing breeds suspicion. Entrepreneurial thinkers thrive on being trusted and appreciated. Firms with a culture of fear only drive these people away. With a feudal mentality, it should be no surprise if the only employees that remain are serfs who simply follow orders. Even the "genius with a thousand helpers" just isn't smart enough to cope with the numerous and unknown variables in today's economy.

3. If sales professionals are not strategically engaged, they are forced to remain peddlers of products. When engaging with clients, they are unaware of the strategically relevant information available to them. Consequently, they focus on what they can sell rather than on what they can learn. These interactions quickly become tedious for clients, and clients keep these vendors at arm's length.

While suppliers must make significant changes to engage clients in this new way, the client must also be familiar and comfortable with this mode of operation and receptive to these new levels of engagement. Not all clients will be ready. You must carefully select those clients in whom you will invest strategic effort. The good news is that increasing client expectations about trust, engagement, and collaboration are pushing this type of relationship front and center.

Stage Five: Symbiotic Partner

At stage five, the relationship has evolved beyond a person-to-person relationship to a business-to-business relationship grounded and defined by the symbiotic partnership. Your company has become an integral part of how your client delivers value to their clients. The relationship is collaborative, which enables you to address current strategic priorities as well as gather insights to anticipate future challenges and opportunities.

At this level, the relationship has evolved from "push" to "pull." You have demonstrated your knowledge and your ability to co-create solutions and provide the client with strategically relevant and creative insights and ideas. The working relationship is highly interdependent and collaborative between the client, your business, suppliers, and other invested stakeholders.

An important aspect of symbiotic partner status is that you must continually re-earn it. The role of symbiotic partner is a dynamic and constantly changing one because the client's business is also dynamic and constantly changing. Your value-add today may no longer be perceived in the same way tomorrow. You must continually look for new value-add solutions to maintain your role as symbiotic partner. This means keeping up with your client's business, their industry, their competitors, and their challenges and staying several steps ahead of them.

Here is a graphic example of how the different aspects of the sales dynamic change with each relationship stage.

	Stranger	Supplier	Desired Supplier	Trusted Advisor	Symbiotic Partner
Selection of Clients	No differentiation between or among clients	Focus on quantity. More transactions = more profitability	Focus on quality—how well clients match ideal profile and how much they are investing in the relationship	Focus on access to internal information, such as strategic plans, decision criteria, etc.	Focus on shared values
Value Delivery	One-size-fits-all approach	Pre-packaged value approach	Customized, collaboratively generated value-add	Value goes beyond supplier's offerings and includes other resources that can deliver on client's objectives	Value delivery is shared between supplier and client and focused on client's customer
Profit	Low	High (but may not be sustainable)	High, with increased sustainability	High, with increasing degrees of control	Very high
Focus	Pushing out value message and value proposition	Delivering on promises	Understanding and exceeding expectations	Pulling in client-relevant information and knowledge	Understanding how to fulfill shifting definition of value for client's customers
Client Knowledge Requirement	Requires minimal client knowledge	Requires surface-level client knowledge	Requires broader client knowledge from multiple sources.	Requires deep client knowledge, client cooperation, and willingness to share	Intuitive understanding of client emerges as a result of shared values, goals, and experiences
Basis of Relationship	Price, utility	Quality/price, reliable transactions	Responsiveness	Trust, respect, advocacy	Mutual gain, common values
Primary Relationship Enabler	Organization (brand)	Individual (personal chemistry)	Organization (processes)	Individual(s) (personal credibility)	Organization (company vision and values)

Table 1. How Sales Dynamics Change with Each Client Relationship Stage

How to Transition to the Next Level

In order to transition to the next client relationship stage, first pay attention to the primary relationship enabler at your current stage. Note from the table above that the movement through relationship stages swings back and forth from individual to organization. At the stranger stage, it is the brand or organization that exerts the most influence. The better known the brand, the more trust there will be in allowing a stranger to sell to us.

To become a supplier, the focus is on the individual. I will entertain you as a stranger because I know the brand. You will become my supplier because I have come to trust you as a person. So it's down to the individual in front of me. People buy from people—people they know, people they like, and people they trust. When becoming a supplier, it is the individual salesperson that is most important. However, salespeople are expensive. More and more companies are trying to figure out how to engage buyers without having to hire salespeople. This is possible only if we are dealing with a commodity. The more a product is commoditized, the less need there is for trust and the less need there is for a salesperson. Furthermore, the intelligence being built into inbound marketing campaigns is enabling companies to make appropriate offers to potential buyers. While this trend continues, the need for humans to have trusted advisors will also continue. Moving beyond the transaction will only be possible when there is real human-to-human contact. If this contact is not made in the initial transaction, it must be made with subsequent interactions.

As we move to desired supplier, it is once again the company that exerts the most influence. As an individual, your salesperson made promises to me. She can't fulfill them all by herself. Now it's the company behind her—its people, processes, and passion—that's going to make me promote your company to a desired supplier. Zappos is an example of a company that has done well selling via e-commerce. While they don't have a sales force, they have invested heavily in customer service. A shoe is a commodity. We will order shoes via the Internet as long as we know we're dealing with a reputable company. However, Zappos has developed a loyal following because of the human touch they provide with their customer service.

To move from desired supplier to trusted advisor, we're back to the individual. IBM is not my trusted advisor—John Smith is my trusted advisor. I pick up the phone and call to talk to John. I have developed a trusted relationship with John.

Trusted advisor status is a huge leap forward. It's difficult to get there but it offers a wonderful advantage. It also comes with risks. Your company is vulnerable because the client's relationship is with a particular sales professional. So if that salesperson decides to leave the company and go with a competitor, chances are the client will go with him. Conversely, if the client contact leaves their company, your trusted advisor status goes out the door with them.

From a corporate perspective, it's important that you develop multiple trusted advisor relationships. The company cannot be overly dependent on any one person or relationship. These relationships are built on the financial investment and support of the company, and they are a company asset. Every ethical sales professional will understand and support this.

Symbiotic partnerships, on the other hand, are strategic alliances between companies. My company is not going to enter into a strategic alliance with John Smith; my company is going to enter into a strategic alliance with IBM. A symbiotic partnership is a corporate-to-corporate agreement.

Get to Work on Trust

If you're like most people, you are trustworthy. After all, you consider yourself honest, virtuous, ethical—a person of good character. Yet you don't have the trusted advisor relationship that you'd like to have with many of your clients. Why is that? Good character is important but unnecessary for building trust. Trust depends on something else.

Think about it. Why is it that gangs enjoy the highest levels of internal trust when compared to other social groups? Hardened criminals who have poor character enjoy more trust with their peers than many practicing religious people. Every week, in most places of worship comprising more than a handful of people, you don't have to look far to find power struggles. It is an exceptional group of people that do not display this dysfunction. Yet among hardened criminals there are high degrees of loyalty. A gang member can be wrongly convicted and will serve time rather than turn in a fellow gang member. Why the discrepancy?

Rather than think of trust as a function of character, we need to see it as a function of something else. That something else is *buy-in*. How much and how deeply do people buy into a vision, a mission, and/or a set of core values? The extent to which there is buy-in is the extent to which there is trust.

Despite the terrible consequences of being involved in gangs, gangs continue to grow. Clearly, of all the bad choices available to the disadvantaged, belonging to a gang is desirable. It fills the emotional tank and satisfies the craving to belong. The high price one pays to belong is a small hurdle when compared to the deep feeling of belonging that is fulfilled. That sense of belonging causes gang members to buy into a code of conduct that says you never "rat someone out." If you become known as a "rat" you no longer belong!

Organizations that suffer from infighting really suffer from a lack of buy-in to a common vision and set of core values.

Use this revised definition of trust to help you build stronger relationships with your family, friends, co-workers, and clients. With respect to your clients:

1. How well do you understand their long-term goals?
2. Do you really buy into their long-term goals?

To the extent that you a) understand and b) buy into their goals, you will create the conditions necessary for trust. You can't fake it. You must really understand and authentically buy into their goals. Any lack of authenticity will eventually bubble to the surface. Not only must the sales professional buy in but the company behind him/her must also buy in. Without company support, the sales professional's buy-in will be shallow.

Be careful not to be inconsistent. Inconsistency is a destroyer of trust. Inconsistency creates unpredictability. When someone is unpredictable, they cannot be trusted. Do the things you say you will do. Develop good habits. Get back to people when you say you will. Always follow through on the things you've promised. If you are aware that something is not going as well as it should, be the first to bring it to your client's attention. Don't wait for them to ask you about it. If you're going to be late, call as soon as you know. Always be courteous. These habitual ways of being will broadcast consistency. Buy-in combined with consistency will create the ideal conditions for trust.

Also, take the time to ensure your whole company shares the same values with respect to clients. Organizations are becoming increasingly permeable. This means that a customer is no longer restricted to talking solely to salespeople. Through various channels (Twitter, blogs, Facebook, LinkedIn, etc.) they can easily engage others deep inside the organization. If their values are not consistent with the salesperson's, trust will be destroyed.

With trust as the foundation, here is how to transition to the next relationship stage with your clients:

From Stranger to Supplier

The key to moving from stranger to supplier lies with brand strength (to get the foot in the door initially) and with the ability of the individual salesperson to demonstrate credibility, build trust, and engage the client. It's important to realize that when you show up as a stranger, your prospective client most likely has a strategic relationship with someone else. This relationship presents a significant barrier for you to get through. Often you can become a supplier by doing a small, seemingly insignificant, low-risk transaction.

From Supplier to Desired Supplier

The move from supplier to desired supplier requires proof that you and your team will go above and beyond to meet the needs of the client. You understand that your client is in the process of expressing a desired idea and you are committed to helping them realize their dream. The client needs to feel they can trust your company and depend on you to deliver. You enhance their reputation—you make them look good!

Again, another critical element here is consistency. Consistency is how the client will begin to trust you and be open to your advice. The only way we can get to desired supplier status and retain that over time is if we have consistency over time. Your organization has to invest in processes, systems, standards, and metrics so that it is able to deliver consistently. That consistency supports the creation of trust. Hence, as we endeavor to move into deeper client relationships, our companies must evolve to become disciplined and systematized. Without the discipline of systems, we are dependent on human discretion, which is anything but consistent.

Relationships are key enablers, and at this stage it means relationships not just with salespeople but with everyone in your organization. In fact, it is at this stage where the culture of your organization begins to have its impact.

Every touch point becomes important because each is an illustration of your company's commitment to serving the client. Client support, marketing, accounting, and other services must offer a genuine and consistent face to the client—one that repeatedly reminds them that you value their business and are there to support them.

One of the key payoffs of having this client-centric approach and supporting culture is that you will move to desired supplier faster.

It's great to achieve desired supplier status, but as we've already established, you can't stop there. The means that got you there—in particular, the operational efficiencies and systemization—are no longer sufficient to keep you ahead of the competition. Why? Because the minute you are able to get everything systematized is the minute it has lost its mystery and can now be packaged, copied, and commoditized.

The complexity has been figured out, it's easy to duplicate, and you've lost your competitive edge.

So what must you do to move to the next level, the level of trusted advisor?

From Desired Supplier to Trusted Advisor

The platform of consistent delivery will build a level of trust that positions you to move into the role of trusted advisor. In order to make this transition, you must focus on further developing the relationship with quality face time and true value-add.

The trusted advisor relationship is twofold. First, it depends on trust. Trust takes time. Therefore, face time is an important element of the relationship. The experience of being face-to-face in each other's space increases trust. Face-to-face interactions with clients give us opportunities to get to know and understand each other. But there must be value associated with the time clients spend with us.

The other aspect of the relationship is the value that comes from the advisory nature of the relationship. This value is provided when you make the shift from content to context. Content is provided when you know your products and/or services. You are the expert. That's good, but it is insufficient to move into a trusted advisor relationship. Context is required.

Context is provided when you know and become an expert in your client's world. If I'm your client, you understand my mission, values, and key players. You know my business and the idiosyncrasies of my situation. You understand what it is I'm trying to achieve, and you are committed to helping me achieve it, with or without your resources.

If you don't understand my business and you try to provide some good ideas, they're just ideas and they will do very little to elevate you to trusted advisor status in my eyes. However, if you have taken the time to really understand my situation and your advice is considered and nuanced, I'm going to attach a lot more weight to what you have to say.

An advisor is in a position of authority. You can never expect to be in a position of authority if you don't understand the nuances of someone's situation. How can I take you seriously if all you have is a superficial understanding of my challenges?

You know you have achieved trusted advisor status when your clients call you and ask you to help them think through their challenges. Their request demonstrates their respect for your business acumen as well as your efforts in getting to know their business. As a general rule, as you move up the relationship continuum, your clients will call you earlier in their decision-making process. Vendors are called after problems are defined. Partners are called to help define problems.

In addition to the great benefits your client gets from a trusted advisor relationship, you are also richly rewarded. First, because you act in your client's best interest, they trust you to make decisions on their behalf. They know that if you have to bring in other suppliers or even some of your competitors to solve a problem for them, you will do so if it is in their best interest. They reward you in the long term for this loyalty.

Another often overlooked benefit of this level of relationship is the value of the insights you gather when you are so close to your client. There are things you see and conversations you hear that your competition will never have access to. These insights put you in a position of really understanding the challenges your client faces and the true value of what your firm can do for them. They also enable you to see patterns and, as your client's world changes, to detect emerging needs.

Sales professionals and chief executives must place a high value on context. Sales professionals must learn to communicate what they understand to their organizations. A great idea is to schedule Lunch n' Learns for the whole company that are hosted by the sales team. At each Lunch n' Learn the sales team should share the context their clients are operating within. Many employees have no idea about the context in which their products/services are used. One of our customers does this on a regular basis with their international sales team. Whenever a team member comes back from an overseas trip, they are required to share what they have learned in terms of their client's strategy, operations and changing environment. Members from

R&D, Product Marketing and Customer Service benefit enormously from the insights shared and the company has consistently grown more valuable to its customers as a result.

Unfortunately, many sales professionals miss this incredible vantage point because neither they nor their CEO understand the value of being so close to a client. Sales professionals also suffer from New Shiny Object syndrome. They get more of a buzz chasing new clients than from sticking with existing clients. For chief executives, rather than trying to figure how you can automate your business to do without salespeople, spend time figuring out how you can help your salespeople deeply understand their customers. If you make the effort to really get to know your clients, you'll be richly rewarded.

From Trusted Advisor to Symbiotic Partner

The current business environment is so complex and dynamic that companies really can't run solo anymore. In the past, one company did everything: they sourced their own raw materials, they processed them into finished goods, and then they marketed these finished goods. But that's not our world today. Today we need partners to help in various areas of our business. We need partners at all levels, and especially at a strategic level. It is this new reality of business that paves the way for your move to symbiotic partner.

To make the transition from trusted advisor to symbiotic partner, you must identify the areas where a strategic relationship can make an appreciable difference to your client's business. Having moved through desired supplier to trusted advisor, you should have the information you need to develop these collaborative strategies.

Your development from stranger to trusted advisor has been predicated on increasing levels of trust. As a "trusted" advisor, you are really trusted. The trust bank account is full. Ideally, you have multiple trusted advisory relationships within your client organization. This high level of trust combined with deep levels of client understanding opens the door to symbiotic partnering.

A symbiotic partnership may have multiple forms. It might be a joint venture where both firms agree to create a separate entity to pursue an opportunity. Or it might be an outsourcing arrangement where the client agrees to completely outsource a function of its business to your firm. There are many variations. The key is that it is a formalized arrangement focused on creating value for the end client. Put simply, a strategic alliance is enterprise-level symbiosis.

Symbiotic Partners Aim to Deliver Value Rather Than Extract Value

One of the primary differentiators between symbiotic partners and other relationships is their focus. Symbiotic partners are continually looking to *deliver* value to each other rather than *extract* value from each other. As a symbiotic partnership, its value is greater than the sum of its parts.

Most people are in business to extract value. One of the most pronounced experiences I had of this reality was at a sales conference for a software firm I worked for. The VP of sales stood in front of a group of about four hundred sales professionals and shouted, "Get out there and get that contract signed. And get it signed on your terms. Get out there and crush your customer!" You're probably reading this and thinking I'm exaggerating. I assure you I'm not. He really said this. The focus of the firm was driving their stock price higher, and we were getting close to quarter end. He needed his sales team to extract money from customers in order to drive the stock price higher!

These business leaders are in business to take money out of the value account rather than add to the value account. They view business as a zero-sum game, where there are always losers and winners. One way to identify where you stand in this respect is to look at how you treat clients when they're in trouble.

If I am focused on extracting value and the client is in trouble, I'm likely to cut and run at the first sign of trouble. If, however, my focus is on creating value, and my account is beginning to wobble, I'm going to go through the effort of understanding what's going on with this client. What is their mission? What's happening in the marketplace they are operating in? What's happening in the industry? What are their strengths and weaknesses? What are the opportunities? And what can I do to help? Who can I introduce them to that might advance them?

Perhaps I'm able to see things they don't see because they're too close to it. Or I'm able to impart intelligence and lessons learned that I've picked up from other companies. Perhaps I've spotted trends and identified opportunity areas that I'm able to see as a result of being "out there" versus living inside the organization.

This is how you earn symbiotic partner status and create strategic alignment in the long term—by truly caring and seeking unique opportunities to create value.

The fact that a company is in trouble doesn't necessitate us running away from them. In fact, it might be a huge opportunity for us to help them in a way that makes a difference and better positions us to move into a role with more impact.

A company in trouble may provide a greater sense of responsibility for the client's success and a greater sense of agency, meaning we don't have to accept things will just happen the way the trend line is going—we can actually act on the environment and change the fate of our clients.

In the past we hoped the client was successful and would take us with them. Now, as a symbiotic partner, we're saying, "What can we do to help make our client successful?" This is a new way of thinking and not one that many companies will embrace easily—which is why it affords those who do significant opportunity.

Here's an example.

One of my clients manufactures hearing aids. They sell these to audiologists who in turn sell them to consumers. The aging Baby Boomers have impacted this industry in a big way. It's growing at a rapid pace. The stigma of wearing a hearing aid is going away. The technology has improved—hearing aids are much smaller and much more capable and intelligent than they used to be. The market has huge potential.

And this isn't lost on the big corporations who have now entered the market and are trying to buy up all these independent audiologists. In fact, the manufacturers themselves are buying up their clients to create a very strong retail presence. So the independent market is being severely eroded. Massive retail chains and manufacturers are taking over, and the little guys are in trouble. A lot of the independents are selling out or closing shop. Those that remain are struggling.

So if you're a manufacturer of hearing aids and you see this independent market in trouble, what do you do? Do you leave the little guys behind and focus on the big guys? Do you buy them out and compete directly with your clients?

Chris Auty, general manager of Unitron UK, decided to take a different approach. He made the commitment to help the independent market—to be loyal to them. His company decided not to sell the latest technology to the national chains. They made a commitment to do whatever they could to give the advantage to the little guys: the struggling independents.

They understood that these small players are technically savvy but not business savvy and that they needed some help growing their business to a level that could compete with the big chains. So they created Unite University—an educational facility and program designed to help the independents grow their business. They invited me and several other resource providers to come in to teach the independents about sales and marketing. And not just teach them but actually work with them to develop their sales and marketing plan and strategy. They invite me back year after year to provide keynotes and consulting to strengthen their clients.

What transpired during our work together was truly inspiring. Chris had been playing with the idea of the independents coming together as a single brand that could compete with the big guys. He had worked on this strategy for two years. He saw an opportunity to develop a united front, a consumer-facing brand, an umbrella brand where all the independents could come together and become the largest retailer of hearing aids in the UK. He knew that if they could do this they would actually be a force to contend with.

But rather than have it be his idea pushed out on the clients, he created the perfect situation for the idea to incubate and be self-discovered, owned, and presented by the group. He was patient and waited until the time was right. Eventually the clients came to him, saying "Couldn't we together become a brand in the marketplace?"

Here's an example where clients were in trouble. Rather than desert a sinking ship, this visionary said, "I'm going to help my clients be successful. I'm going to educate them on how to be effective at sales and marketing and help them create a brand that gives them some heft in the marketplace." Think about the loyalty he has engendered among these clients! It's huge, and it will be very difficult for other manufacturers to penetrate.

It's easy to imagine how this scenario might play out in a typical organization that did not have a clear focus of adding value for clients and an open mind about how to get there. Imagine proposing this idea in a less supportive culture or a less client-focused culture. Chris Auty was successful because he had Cameron Hay as his CEO. Cam had the values and vision that were supportive of his approach. Many CEOs would not have the patience or vision to support Chris's strategy. The same person with the same strategy would fail in an unsupportive environment. Unitron is clear on why it's in business, and this focus guides and enables decisions like this. The mantra you have to remember is simply this: we are in business to create value for our clients.

Right Fit versus Poor Fit

To achieve sales symbiosis, we seek to align our companies with our right-fit clients. Understanding the process of the client relationship helps us to define our perfect client, but it also drives home the importance of working with the right fit. It is not a matter of leaving some out of the possibility of being a client, but understanding that only a few will rise to the level of a symbiotic partner. The 80/20 rule again applies: only 20 percent of clients might move all the way up the relationship curve to become symbiotic partners, but they are the ones that will provide 80 percent of the company's profitability.

As we recognize a right fit and a poor fit, we can streamline our interactions with clients: we continue to be who we are and do what we do, but we do it differently for different clients, respecting each type.

Now that we've built the foundation of understanding the history of client relationships and the symbiotic client relationship lifecycle, Part 2 will explain the symbiotic sales strategy step-by-step. As with our understanding of the five stages of client relationships, we must learn to take the client's point of view. We need to shift our selling strategy to follow the buying cycle.

CEO Action Plan

❐ Segment your customers based on how *they* view their relationship with you.

❐ Identify those customers who deserve more of your attention and those who deserve less.

❐ Update your CRM database with the key goals, priorities, and initiatives of your key customers.

❐ Ensure that your people understand how your goods and services enable your key customers to reach their goals.

Sales Professional Action Plan

❐ Practice listening for the desires of people around you in your personal and professional life.

❐ Document the long-term goals of your clients and prospective clients.

❐ Document the value beyond the transaction you give and receive from your clients.

❐ Host an internal Lunch n' Learn and share your contextual understanding of your clients with your work colleagues. Ensure they really understand the context of your clients.

PART THREE

THE HUMAN-TO-HUMAN
ENTERPRISE: GROWING UP

Chapter 11

THE HUMAN-TO-HUMAN ENTERPRISE LIFECYCLE: THE FIVE STAGES OF COMPANY DEVELOPMENT

You've got to be very careful if you don't know
where you're going, because you might not get there.
—Yogi Berra

As we pointed out in Part One, when the center of your universe changes, everything changes. In the Industrial Age we defined and prepackaged the value for our clients. We then set out to persuade and convince the client it was right for them. And we structured our enterprises accordingly. Industrial Age businesses lost the human touch. They were impersonal and aggressive.

Now that our center of gravity has shifted from our definition of value to the right-fit client's definition of value, the structure of our enterprise must also change. Now that we've established what human-to-human selling looks like, what does the human-to-human enterprise look like?

Generally speaking, with the right-fit client at the center, the human-to-human enterprise will structure itself according to the following basic assumptions: (1) change is a constant, and (2) both systems thinking and innovation are required to build a scalable business and to serve humans well.

Change Is a Constant

Rather than the product-push of the Industrial Age, clients want *solutions*. Solutions must be created dynamically for each client. We can no longer afford to push "one-size-fits-all" or prepackaged products. Although we've come a long way from Henry Ford's "they can have any color they like as long as it's black," we still expect our clients to make sacrifices in order to make our products or services work for them. Idiosyncratic preferences are inconvenient to us. Changing preferences are inconvenient to us. If we had things our way, we would design algorithms for every aspect of production and set up assembly lines and cheap labor to turn out lots of product. Every time an important client's preferences change, we need to modify our assembly line. Every time an algorithm is challenged, we need to hire expensive, thinking labor. Just as we find our stride, the pace or direction of the race changes. As it changes, those who can't deal with complexity put their head in the sand. Those who can keep their head up and pick up the pace.

Not only has the source of our definition of value changed, but perceptions of value are also rapidly changing. Where once we could create the right products and rest on our laurels, now we must constantly re-evaluate our value proposition. Value is just a perception, and perceptions can change in an instant. American writer and philosopher Eric Hoffer said, "In times of change, learners inherit the earth, while the learned find themselves beautifully equipped to deal with a world that no longer exists."

This one quote captures the inherent danger of systematization. The algorithms developed during the systematization process are based on paradigms that, in a shifting world, may no longer be true.

Both Systems Thinking and Innovation Are Required to Serve Humans Well

As we systematize business and introduce necessary discipline, we often inadvertently create an environment that is hostile to entrepreneurial individuals but attractive to "professional managers."

Professional managers are great at implementing order and enforcing compliance. This talent presupposes a known and understood environment. Professional managers may flounder in complexity and uncertainty, while complexity and uncertainty is where entrepreneurs thrive. Entrepreneurs, however, may flounder when it comes to creating consistency and order. Without consistency and order, no business can survive. Both types of thinking are required.

As we systematize our solutions and business processes, we need to figure out how to retain the entrepreneurial talent that exists in our organizations. In the new world, we need to manage our businesses as two separate businesses: OldCo, or the part of our business that can be reduced to an algorithm and therefore can be systematized, and NewCo, the part of our business that responds to new challenges and opportunities.[7] Just as businesses and right-fit clients need each other, so do entrepreneurs and managers—even though at times it's an uneasy romance. Appreciating and integrating the skills of both, and thus creating a human-to-human enterprise, is reflected in a perspective known as *design thinking*.

The Knowledge Funnel

According to Roger Martin, dean at the Rotman School of Business in Toronto and an expert on design thinking in business, knowledge

---

7   Roger Martin has produced an influential body of work on design in business, showing that successful innovation is not a random mystery but requires a deliberate integration of creative thinking and analytical thinking through a process known as the *knowledge funnel*. See his classic article "The Design of Business," *Rotman Magazine*, Winter 2004, as well as his books *The Design of Business: Why Design Thinking Is the Next Competitive Advantage* (Harvard Business School Press, 2009) and *The Opposable Mind: Winning through Integrative Thinking* (Harvard Business School Press, 2009).

comes into our organizations through a funnel.[8] At the top of the funnel, something is a mystery. It forces us to ask questions. As we begin to figure it out, we form rules of thumb or heuristics. Once the rules of thumb become better understood, we are able to convert our knowledge into an algorithm. Algorithms allow us to hire cheap labor to do repetitive tasks. Systems thinking lives with algorithms.

Innovation deals with mystery and heuristics. Innovation requires far greater cognitive faculties and never shies away from new data, no matter how disruptive it may be. Systems managers must be great analysts. Innovation managers must be synthesists, possessing the ability to put information together in new and creative ways. This ability to synthesize is what enables them to spot and create opportunities before anyone else.

Once we understand that our business is comprised of both systems and innovation, we can become proactive about change. We can gather information about how the world of our key clients is changing, and we can anticipate their emerging needs and changing priorities. We can then collaborate with them proactively to figure out how to address their new challenges. The systems part of our business is about following and repeating a known but rapidly aging success formula. The innovation part of the business is more about sensing and responding to our changing landscape. There is no algorithm because there are too many unknowns.

The Symbiotic Enterprise Lifecycle

Like people, businesses go through stages to get to maturity. To draw a parallel with how we mature in our relationships, the more mature I am, the healthier the relationships I'll have. The more mature my enterprise is, the healthier our relationships will be. If I am a seventeen-year-old in a committed relationship, it's not likely I'll be

---

8   Roger Martin, *The Design of Business: Why Design Thinking Is the Next Competitive Advantage* (Harvard Business School Press, 2009), 7-9.

in that relationship five years later because my immaturity puts me in a needier place—as opposed to a person who is more mature, less needy, more giving, and thus more capable of sustaining a longer-term relationship.

Historically, businesses needed to go through these three stages before coming to maturity:

Stage	Focus	Potential Problems
A. The Entrepreneurial Enterprise	Creativity, trial, and error	Cash flow
B. The Performing Enterprise	Developing methods and procedures that enable repeatability	Key people get stretched too thin, burn out, let customers down
C. The Systematic Enterprise	Economies of scale	Poorly designed systems (not achieving the systems payoff) Not moving forward (not moving out of the systematic phase when you need to)

The Age of Reformation has changed everything, and now to succeed businesses must pass through an additional two stages before being considered mature and fully ready for human-to-human selling.

The focus and potential problems of these two additional stages differ from the previous three:

ENTERPRISE LIFECYCLE

ENTREPRENEURIAL	PERFORMING	SYSTEMATIC	ADAPTIVE	PREEMPTIVE
A	**B**	**C**	**D**	**E**

Figure 10.1. The Enterprise Lifecycle

Stage	Focus	Potential Problems
D. The Adaptive Enterprise	Detecting new competitive threats	Responding to threats too late
E. The Preemptive Enterprise	Developing a thorough understanding of best-fit customers Collaborating with customers Co-developing solutions with best-fit customers	Focusing on and investing too much in the wrong customers

Stage A: The Entrepreneurial Enterprise (Newborn)

Every business, no matter how great, starts with an individual and an idea. It takes a certain type of person, armed with little more than an idea, to begin a company. Entrepreneurs are visionaries. They see what others don't. Typically, they are not very practical. Starting a business from scratch is not a practical thing to do. It often takes much longer than expected to get the business off the ground, and it often costs much more than anticipated. Eighty percent of new businesses fail within the first five years. These minor details do not deter entrepreneurs. They are fueled by their vision. Reality is a minor inconvenience. They use their spiritual and emotional energy to create a new reality.

Meeting people's needs also fuels them. They stay close to their clients and they bend over backward to help them. Even if the request is irrelevant to the rest of the company's clients, entrepreneurs go out of their way to please.

The entrepreneur is driven by the belief that building a better mousetrap is the secret to success. While cash flow is day-to-day, the entrepreneur pushes on and is rewarded by the thrill rather than the till. The lack of cash flow, however, forces the entrepreneurial company to take any client they can get regardless of whether or not the client is a right-fit or a poor-fit client.

Stage B: The Performing Enterprise (Toddler)

At this stage the company finds its legs. It has a real value proposition, and clients want what it is selling. It begins to invoice according to the value of the product, and clients acknowledge the value. Its focus, however, moves from each individual client to a market. The company learns how to say no to client requests.

The Performing Enterprise depends on the performance of key individuals. These "A" players are as passionate as the founder, and they have fully bought into the mission of the company. The Performing Enterprise may also have B and C players on board. As the company continues to grow, it outgrows them. They were needed when the company was floundering; however, they've become attached to the founder and it becomes difficult to break the sense of personal loyalty in the relationship.

The heroic efforts of the "A" players wow clients and keep the company afloat. Because these "A" players are so hard to find, it is not long before they get stretched too thin. The more stretched they become, the more they realize they need to add new people.

Adding new people takes time and requires training. It becomes a vicious cycle. The more stretched they become, the more they guard their time. It is faster for them to do things themselves than take the time to train others who will never do it as well as they can. Between the A players being stretched thin and the B and C players not pulling their weight, the company begins to wobble.

Eventually the company takes on one too many clients and the A players can no longer cope. Delivery dates begin to slip, quality deteriorates, response times lengthen, and a host of other symptoms emerge which begin to turn off clients.

Eventually the entrepreneur realizes help is needed.

Stage C. The Systematic Enterprise (Teenager)

The move from Performing to Systematic is such a big jump that it typically requires different people to take on leadership roles. I call these people professional managers. Professional managers come from large companies. Unlike the entrepreneur, they are very practical people. They appreciate order and they possess the ability to impose it. Everything in its place and a place for everything is their mantra. They bring the experience of discipline in strategy, operations, finance, marketing, sales, purchasing, human resource management, and every other area of business. They know how things should be done. They introduce the systems and processes necessary for growth and consistency.

At this stage in the company's growth, the founder often loses credibility. Although the founder came up with the original idea and weathered the storms to get the company where it is, all the chaos that plagues the company at this stage permeated the company on the founder's watch. When the professional managers arrive, they arrive with impressive resumes and incredible know-how. They fix things. In fact, they fix everything. They work their magic. The founder is forced to admit the company outgrew him or her and acknowledge the organizational prowess of the professional manager.

A noticeable exception to founders being unable to scale their businesses is Bayard Winthrop, founder of American Giant, a clothing manufacturer. Bayard was a business consultant before starting American Giant in 2012. Unlike many founders, he planned scalability into his business. Success came quickly. As a result of some free publicity, the company was inundated with orders and was temporarily thrown off kilter despite planning for scalability. Fortunately, they were able to adapt, and they are currently forecasting growth of 500 percent.

From Adhocracy to Bureaucracy

Systems take on a much bigger role in the company, and for some of the original employees the environment is no longer fun. It is no longer a case of "flying by the seat of their pants" with the associated adrenaline rush, but filling out form 13456-A when something needs to be done. There is a process to handle any situation that might arise, and management is in place to develop those systems and see they are maintained.

The founding employees enjoy adhocracy and despise bureaucracy. They are people of action. They don't understand why forms must be filled out before action can be taken. When they take action without filling out the appropriate forms, they get their hands slapped. Work is no longer fun. They miss the frequent adrenaline rushes. They find the routine of systems and processes boring, and they no longer feel valued. Often at this stage the founder leaves with some of the key employees to find work in a more entrepreneurial environment. They acknowledge that they can no longer work in such a structured environment.

Typically, professional managers emphasize the reduction of risk. They want repeatability and predictability. Entrepreneurs, on the other hand, are risk takers. They stick their neck out on a hunch and then seek validation. Validation costs money, takes time, and exists in the future. Repeatability is based on the past. This is why professional managers and entrepreneurs often clash.

While having dinner with a colleague whose wife is an anesthesiologist, he explained the relationship between a doctor and an anesthesiologist in such a way that parallels the relationship between an entrepreneur and a professional manager.

He used the example of open-heart surgery: "Adrian, do you realize that the doctor is actually trying to kill the patient? Think about it! Anyone who uses a saw to cut through your ribcage is trying to kill you. The anesthesiologist is trying to keep the patient alive by delivering a precise cocktail of drugs that prevent the body from going into shock. The anesthesiologist is putting the patient to sleep, the most restful state of the body."

Entrepreneurs and professional managers are the same. Professional managers are trying to put the company on autopilot so that everything will run smoothly and consistently. The entrepreneur is constantly shaking up the status quo and putting the company at risk with new ideas.

Traditional professional managers view entrepreneurial ideas with suspicion. More often than not, these ideas have no historical basis. They are future-oriented and based on a hunch. Professional managers are past-oriented and fact-based. Professional managers love data and reports. Entrepreneurs love gut feeling. If the conflict is unresolved, professional managers usually win.

Despite the undisciplined nature of the entrepreneur, his or her departure can be devastating to the organization. Historically, systematization was the final stage of maturity. Because demand was consistent and could be taken for granted, businesses needed to focus on preparing for scalability and minimizing risk. Unlike the Performing Enterprise, the Systematic Enterprise is not people-dependent. When people leave, they are easily replaced because of the documented systems and effective training provided.

There is, however, one glaring exception to this. When people, usually the founder, take the entrepreneurial spirit out of the company, the Systematic Enterprise will eventually die. It lacks the ability to skate to where the puck is going because the people running the company are past-oriented. They rely on proof, and proof is found in the past. Professional managers are often like the driver that tries to drive forward by looking through the rearview mirror. Most of the metrics professional managers study are lagging indicators and point to what happened rather than what will happen. In a fast-changing world, the Systematic Enterprise eventually loses its creative soul and inevitably becomes irrelevant to clients, offering nothing more than unnecessary overhead and the associated high prices. Clients question its value, as do employees and investors.

Systematization is critical to the success of companies as its absence leads to inconsistent performance. Inconsistent performance destroys trust. When you live in an environment day in and day out, you stop seeing what is around you. When we come into an organization to do an audit, we scrutinize everything that can impact client relationships and are quickly able to detect systemic flaws that obstruct sales growth and/or jeopardize trust in client relationships.

The implementation of effective systems is critical to success but it is insufficient. Systematization serves as a foundation for growth. It is not the end game. If you are building a company for your clients, as your clients change, your company must be ready to change. The key to this kind of growth is not systematization but adaptation. However, the adaptation must be based on client insights. Client insights will only come if you are able to get close enough to your clients. You can only get close to your clients if you don't let them down.

We are constantly surveying chief executives on behalf of our clients. One of the questions we often ask is "What does it take for someone to become your trusted advisor"? Among the answers we consistently get back are "Be dependable. Prove to me that I can rely on you. Don't let me down." The only way you can be sure not to let your client down is if you have systems behind you that provide consistent performance.

Trisura Guarantee Insurance Company, a Canadian-based property and casualty insurance company, understands this. Trisura was founded with a core philosophy to excel in the technical aspects of underwriting insurance and to be trusted advisors to their clients. They do not try to be all things to all brokers. Instead they have set clear criteria for what an ideal broker partner looks like. They limit the number of partners they do business with to enable them to provide superior service and customer delight. Trisura invests heavily in systems and processes to ensure consistent customer experiences.

It's a virtuous cycle. Systematization builds trust. Trust opens the door to client intimacy, and client intimacy produces client insights. Insights lead to meaningful adaptation. You can't have meaningful adaptation without first having systematization.

When was the last time you looked at your organization's sales practices with fresh eyes? It's amazing what you stop seeing when you live in the same environment every day. Take the time to do an audit and see your organization through your clients' eyes.

But today's rapidly changing environment requires another transition: a transition to the Adaptive Enterprise.

Stage D: The Adaptive Enterprise (Young Adult)

Today's successful company cannot afford the arrogance of yesterday, believing that clients will remain loyal because they have been in the past, or that the value proposition provided in the past will remain relevant in the future. The danger of systematization is that systems can become impersonal and obsolete. It is also difficult for systems to continually deliver customer delight over time. Opportunities for customer delight come from unexpected opportunities. To continue to be successful, organizations must leave a portion of their resources to react to the things they do not expect.

Cadbury has a long history of being a successful chocolatier in England, but a few years ago it suddenly found that sales of Cadbury chocolates had dropped off dramatically in the shops that serviced schoolchildren. What was the problem? Had schoolchildren suddenly become more conscientious about their treats? Hardly.

Upon further investigation, the company found that the introduction of mobile phones and calling cards meant that tweens (early teens) were now spending their money on phone cards instead of chocolates. The best market planning could not have prepared for this; only an Adaptive Enterprise can react to a blindside competitor—competitors or market forces that come out of left field. More and more, business leaders are finding themselves competing with all the traditional competitors plus competitors that come out of completely different industries. New competitors, new technologies, and changes in the environment such as terrorist attacks, collapsing economies, and/or demographic shifts can all impact the perception of your clients and your relationship with them. Fortunately, once Cadbury recognized their competitors were no longer just other candy manufacturers but any company that vied for tweens' income, they adapted by broadening their marketing approach.[9]

What is it about your company and your products or services that clients really value? What is the outcome they are pursuing? Can you react to the clients' shifting definition of what gives value to your product?

If you can that's great, but it's not enough.

Stage E: The Preemptive Enterprise (Mature Adult)

Today's successful company must do everything that companies of the past did and more. Simply adapting to shifting perceptions of value, however, is not enough because adaptation is reactive. Successful companies must be able to anticipate emerging changes in client priorities and proactively set the agenda for their industry. In the past, a company would hope that its latest idea would last long enough in the marketplace for the next great idea to come along. Today, it is not enough to have great new products and create a demand for them through the marketing department. Today, as in the Age of the Artisan, we must have deep relationships with our clients; we must really know them and be able to anticipate emerging needs before the clients even recognize it.

Being a Preemptive Enterprise is more than listening to clients as they tell you what they would like you to do for them. If Henry Ford had listened to his clients' requests, he would have bred horses that ran faster and for longer periods of time. That may have worked for the Pony Express, but it was not what the client of the early 1900s really needed. They needed faster, more reliable transportation, and Henry Ford developed a way to do that with his early automobiles. Then, as his

9   Thanks to journalist Les Kletke for sharing the story about Cadbury's adaptation.

company grew through the stages of maturity, it developed systems of mass production that brought down the unit cost of production. In fact, in many ways Henry Ford was the founder of systematization with his revolutionary assembly line model.

Ford is often quoted as saying "A client can have a Model T in any color he wants, as long as it's black." What is often left out is the explanation that followed: black paint dried faster than the other colors of paint because of the pigment used in them. The slower drying period for other colors meant fewer cars could be produced on the assembly line, and that drove up cost. Ford was willing to meet the clients' demands, but he also understood what the client really needed—and a lower-priced car was more important than a lime green or navy blue car. The Model T was produced in black because Ford understood the emerging needs of his clients! Our modern example is Steve Jobs. He said customers can have any color iPhone they want as long as its black or white. He understood that customers had higher priorities than the color. Customers were happy to buy colored vanity cases for their phones, which meant Jobs was able to take cost out of production, increase margin, and increase speed to market. Other manufacturers were constrained by the wide variety of models they offered to their customers. They couldn't compete with Apple because they didn't have the operational efficiencies nor the profit margins Apple enjoyed.

The human-to-human enterprise positions itself to repeatedly predict what clients will value next. Unlike traditional companies that invest heavily in R&D to create new products, Preemptive Enterprises collaborate with their clients to ensure new products and services will really be valuable. Epson is another great example of this.

Epson realizes that many in the aging Boomer population are going to end up as dementia patients. In anticipation of developing technologies to address this societal shift, it asked families of people already suffering from dementia if anthropologists from the company could spend time living with them to better understand the challenges they face and to develop products that address their specific issues.

Notice that Epson did not ask these families what technologies it should develop. It wanted to understand its customers at the level of their personal experience and desired outcomes. It asked these families if they would allow them access to their world, to see how caregivers and people who have dementia see the world. The answer was a resounding yes, and Epson not only obtained valuable research data for developing new products, it is building a relationship with the families of those impacted by the disease.

This approach requires that we decide up front which clients are "right-fit clients" and which are not. The Preemptive Enterprise focuses on building relationships with strategic clients who value them. Poor-fit clients are treated transactionally or encouraged to take their "patronage" to better suited companies. Unlike the Entrepreneurial Enterprise, the Preemptive Enterprise does not try to be all things to all people. It focuses its creative and entrepreneurial resources on those clients that value what it offers.

Is Every Stage Necessary?

I'm often asked, can some of these stages be skipped? The answer is no. Each stage contains lessons that must be learned for the firm to properly mature into the next stage. Each stage of development in a company's maturity is a necessary foundation for the subsequent stage. In fact, in the first three stages, each stage replaces its predecessor. It is imperative that firms go through every stage.

While the first three stages are actual transitions, the last two are additions. That is to say, when a company becomes systematic, it never relinquishes systematization. It builds on it. Rather than implementing systems for the convenience and scalability of the company, it relentlessly implements systems that create valuable customer experiences. It realizes that its systems are the flipside of customer experience.

I always find myself somewhere between amusement and annoyance when I call my cell phone company and I'm asked to key in my ten-digit cell phone number. When I'm finally routed to an operator that can address my concern, inevitably the first thing I'm asked is what my ten-digit cell phone number is. It becomes obvious that keying in that number was not for my convenience but for theirs. This is an example of inadequate systematization.

Adaptation and symbiosis do not replace but rather are built upon systematization. This is where the founding employees can continue to shine. While their initial know-how must be documented and reduced to algorithms to grow, they needn't fear being replaced by machines or cheap labor. Their instincts, courage, and insights are required for the company to forge new paths in the adaptive and symbiotic stages.

The adaptive stage is perhaps the most crucial as it is in this stage that the intellectual minds learn to coexist with the intuitive minds and vice versa. Most companies self-destruct because of the internal conflict that arises with significant change. The Adaptive Enterprise learns to embrace change and value the multiple types of personalities and thinking styles. As they master their ability to embrace change, they put themselves in a position to seize new opportunities that competitors are unable to exploit due to internal politics and personal fears.

The final two stages do not replace their predecessors; they build on them. Stages 3, 4, and 5 coexist within a company, with new innovations moving from stages 4 and 5 into stage 3 where they can be systematized and delivered with less expensive resources.

Right-Fit Solutions

Another important aspect of plotting these stages of company growth is applying appropriate solutions to your business. People, especially consultants, naturally assume that because a solution worked well for one company, it will automatically work well for all companies. Understanding your company's stage of maturity will help you avoid costly mistakes. New shoes are great and attractive, but if they are too small or too big, they will give you blisters and make it painful for you to move forward.

For example, an Entrepreneurial Enterprise needs to be much more tactical and opportunistic in its pursuit of new sales. Implementing CRM solutions or long-term strategic sales processes can be fatal to these companies. On the other hand, Performing Enterprises that try to implement more formalized processes to become systematic without the required infrastructure will find that they quickly revert back to old habits.

Communication Issues

Understanding where your company is in the lifecycle is also important to mitigate communication issues. Professional managers tend to speak in financial terms (return on investment, internal rate of return, contribution margin, etc.). Entrepreneurs tend to speak in terms related to customer value. These are two different languages and often require a translation service for real understanding to occur. This can be especially difficult in acquisitions or mergers where one company is systematic in nature and acquires or merges with a company that is entrepreneurial in nature. Suddenly the entrepreneurs find themselves in what they can only consider a hostile environment. Many feel disgruntled and begin to disengage. The energy that characterized the organization dissipates and the acquirer starts to wonder why they made the acquisition in the first place.

Entrepreneurs possess the magic of mission. They are consistently told that what they are setting out to do is impossible. They are unbowed by the lack of vision in others. They press on and their depth of belief inspires others to help them. What appears impossible, they make possible. They bring their vision into being. This is done through the energy that comes from their passion and belief. When reality looks bleak, entrepreneurs have the unique ability to ignore it and press on with their belief in the future.

Professional managers possess the magic of margin. What they do was once considered inconceivable. Consider putting the color purple in clothing. This was once such an expensive process that only kings could afford to wear it. It became associated with royalty. As I write this, I see a family with a young girl wearing the color purple. It's not even her best outfit. It's just a casual outfit. Reducing the cost of this process so that purple clothing can be sold to anyone inexpensively, and the manufacturer can still be profitable, is magic. It's the magic of margin. Professional managers know how to take an unprofitable organization and systematize it so that it becomes profitable. They are confident in their abilities because of their past successes. Let them work their magic and all will be well.

In a crisis, entrepreneurs want to seize the reins and work their magic. The problem is that professional managers don't understand their magic and they have their own magic, which doesn't seem like magic to them—just good managerial sense. Neither side understands the magic of the other, and this creates incredible tension and the potential for real conflict.

But as we said earlier, just as businesses and right-fit clients need each other, so do entrepreneurs and professional managers. Understanding where a company has been, where it is, and where it is going on the enterprise life cycle will enable the leaders and their teams to appreciate the special attributes that each brand of magic brings to the organization.

Company Culture

There's a hidden problem in the systematization of organizations. Systematization is attractive because it's the key to scalability. What many leaders don't anticipate, however, is the extent to which systematization can erode a company's culture. In a very real way, systematization is about mechanizing a company's operations. Mechanization, if we are not careful, can be synonymous with dehumanization. Systems lack judgment. Systems lack souls. Systems are algorithms. Computers without the aid of human intervention can run algorithms.

Professional managers tend to be left-brain dominant in their thinking. Entrepreneurs tend to be right-brain dominant in their thinking. Both types of thinking are critical to success, and everyone thinks with their whole brain. Professional managers as well as entrepreneurs employ both types of thinking. However, each has their preference for a style of thinking—especially when under pressure. I realize I am painting both types at their extreme ends. In reality, people are a combination of thinking styles. For clarity, it's good to think of the two styles at their extremes.

Traditional business schools and the traditional corporate community highly prize left-brain, linear thinking. In my opinion, while both styles of thinking are critical to success, one must follow the other. I believe right-brain thinking should lead and left-brain thinking should follow. Right-brain thinking is concerned with meaning, connection, and context. Left-brain thinking is concerned with order, procedure, and categorization. Something must exist first before it can be categorized. When the entrepreneurial spark leaves an organization, the meaningful relevance of the organization tends to decline. The organization becomes a place focused on activity. Activity is critical to success, but only if the activity is meaningful and valued. The right brain has the innate ability to sense meaning and relevance, but it lacks the ability to work with defined structures. As a result, it lacks the ability of the left brain to impose the structure that will lead to success.

What both sides need to understand is this:

- There is no mission without margin.
- There is no sustainable margin without mission.

Margin only exists because someone values what you are doing enough to pay a premium for it. Systems and processes must be constantly scrutinized to confirm that they are in fact perceived as relevant and meaningful.

To say this another way, horsepower is only valuable if we first have a horse. However, having a horse isn't valuable unless the horse can be tamed. Entrepreneurs bring the horses to an organization. Professional managers bring the ability to tame the horses so they can do meaningful work. Entrepreneurs also bring the uncanny ability to know when to switch horses. Professional managers will often wait until it's too late before realizing a new horse is needed.

CRM as Digital Nervous System

In order to integrate the magic of both entrepreneurs and managers to create real value for our clients, we must develop a digital nervous system that enables us to see and hear what's going on with our clients. OldCo must become adept at gathering client information. NewCo must be adept at synthesizing and interpreting client data.

A significant part of systematization should be the implementation of a customer relationship management (CRM) system. CRM enables organizations to capture and categorize their customer knowledge to help them better serve their customers.

I began selling CRM solutions in 1996. I was one of the early evangelists for CRM. Years later I worked for a company that was using one of the systems I used to sell. I was horrified when I saw how underutilized the system was. Since moving into consulting, where we help our clients implement CRM solutions, I've seen repeated situations of underutilization of CRM technology. Why the discrepancy between the promise and the practice?

I think there is one underlying, fundamental reason for the poor implementation of CRM. Ready? It's intention. That's it. One word with a huge meaning.

Most organizations implement CRM as if it were sales force automation (SFA). SFA was big in the 1980s, and its purpose was to help the sales force sell more stuff to more people. It quickly lost favor with the introduction of CRM because business leaders intuitively understood that it was better to have everyone who touches a client work from the same client record. Companies switched from SFA to CRM but their underlying thinking didn't change. Despite the explosion of CRM software capabilities, many companies have done little more than automate their salespeople's Rolodexes. The implementation of CRM was still about selling more stuff to more people.

You can find the evidence to support this claim by simply looking at how CRM solutions are implemented. For the most part, they are glorified address books with sales opportunity information attached. I don't want to negate the value of having up-to-date client information that everyone can access. Nor do I want to negate the value of more accuracy in knowing the value and stage of sales opportunities. My point is that this is not what CRM technology is about.

In my opinion, your CRM is the most strategic software you can implement in your business. The purpose of CRM is to create more value for the firm's clients and prospective clients through an improved relationship. All relationships improve with greater knowledge. Tracking sales opportunity information is our way of knowing how well our efforts to educate our clients are going. What about the flipside? How well are we growing in our knowledge of our clients?

Those CEOs that understand the strategic value of client relationships and client knowledge are passionate and impatient when it comes to using their CRM. They become unreasonable in their demands to get the system up and running well. They ensure they have champions who are passionate about accurate and complete data. They force compliance because they know that the company's ability to create value completely depends on its ability to understand its clients.

When used effectively, CRM will provide a 360-degree view of our clients. We will grow in our understanding, as everyone who touches a client and learns about that client will contribute to the collective understanding of the client.

Over time, not only will we understand each client better, but also we will detect trends in client segments. This will lead to more effective marketing. We'll also understand our clients at a more strategic level, which in turn will lead to improved corporate strategy.

On the marketing front, CRM enables one-to-one communication. Rather than simply sending generalized, broadcast messages to everyone in the database, well-structured CRM systems enable us to send highly targeted and relevant communications to dynamically generated segments of our database. You'll be able to send the right message to the right person at just the right time. The result? You'll begin to have meaningful dialogue with human beings. You will be perceived as helpful rather than intrusive. You will create more value.

CRM should be a company philosophy, not just a technology. Salespeople should be adept at developing strategic client relationships and facilitating the exchange of proprietary information. Imagine the relationship when the salesperson comes back from visiting a key client, saying, "I've uncovered a new emerging need at a key client, and I've gained agreement for our top executives to meet with their top executives to discuss this further." The client now can view a visit from the salesperson as something positive: time spent with a symbiotic partner that provides answers rather than expenses and piercing questions rather than assumptions.

The human-to-human enterprise understands that managers and innovators are not adversaries but right-fit partners when put in the right environment that takes advantage of both skill sets. In the final chapter, we will explore what happens when we overlay the client relationship stages covered in previously with the various enterprise stages from this chapter. Symbiosis happens when both client and supplier are mature: in the Winners' Quadrant.

CEO Action Plan

❏ Assess the maturity of your business processes to determine where you are in the enterprise life cycle.

❏ Determine the job functions that must be eliminated or created for you to get to the next level.

❏ Develop profiles for the job functions that are critical to your future success.

❏ Profile your people and new recruits to ensure you are putting the right people in the right positions.

❏ Make your people aware of where your company is in its lifecycle and how and why both the entrepreneurial and managerial mindsets must be valued.

Sales Professional Action Plan

❏ Develop your thinking skills. Read widely. Converse with a wide variety of people.

❏ Think about where your clients are on the Enterpise Life Cycle. Brainstorm ideas on how you can help them advance.

❏ Commit to mastering your CRM in order to provide superior customer service.

Chapter 12

THE WINNERS' QUADRANT

Winning takes talent; to repeat takes character.
—John Wooden

Businesses today are trapped in a competitive world racing fervently to build the better mousetrap. They are focused on making their existing product smaller, faster, or cheaper. Everyone is trying to do the same thing, and no one has an advantage for any significant time. Business leaders spend more time looking over their shoulder than they do concentrating on the needs of their clients.

The traditional value chain begins with a corporation purchasing assets and then raw materials and using their assets to process the raw materials into finished products. These products are delivered through the various sales channels to the client. The client is the ultimate user of the product but traditionally was not consulted as to what they want or more importantly what their emerging needs might be.

The Preemptive Enterprise starts with the client and works backwards to a product or service that will serve the client's most pressing and emerging needs. It is time to make the shift from inside out, or trying to sell clients on what we want to make, to an approach that is outside-in.

Research on a wide range of innovation projects over a ten-year period by Larry Keeley of Doblin[10] shows that money spent on R&D is often not spent where it will give the best return.

Keeley breaks down innovation efforts into ten areas that he groups into three categories: configuration, offering, and experience. The ten areas are profit model, network, structure, processes, product performance, product system, service, channel, brand and customer engagement (see Figure 11.1). The configuration category focuses on the business model, the offering category focuses on the product and processes, and the experience category focuses on improving the client experience. Most companies invest in the second category: improving their product and processes.

Figure 11.1. The Ten Types of Innovation.
Courtesy of Doblin (www.doblin.com).

Keeley's results far outstrip the Pareto Principle. While the majority of innovation projects focused on product improvement, very few of these projects produced any appreciable return.

In fact, Keeley found that less than 2 percent of all the innovation projects he studied over the ten-year period produced a whopping 90 percent of the value. All the projects in that less-than-2 percent category had one thing in common: they all focused on the business model and the client experience, not just product enhancement. Most businesses are in a furious but misguided race to make a better

---

10   Thanks to Larry Keeley of Doblin, a design-driven innovation consultancy, for permission to reference this study in this book.

product while what really matters is the client's experience and their business model.

In his consulting work, Keeley stresses four main areas that will provide the atmosphere for a business to be innovative enough to get to the front of the competitive pack:

1. Enable an innovation by providing an atmosphere in the business that encourages innovation and innovative thinking.

2. Collaborate with clients, suppliers, and other businesses, whether they are across the street or around the world. Collaboration introduces new ideas and new ways to see the challenges of the future.

3. Focus on talent, whether it is attracting talented people or maintaining them as a part of the operation; this is one of the areas where he sees the greatest real competition.

4. Metrics: the traditional methods of measurement no longer apply. While he stresses the value of measurement, he suggests that new systems of measurement must be in place for the innovation of the future.

Today's value chain begins with the client, and the more you understand the client and their needs, the better.

The Four Quadrants

Eariler, we examined the client relationship life cycle and the enterprise life cycle. When we place these two lifecycles on top of each other, we form a matrix with four quadrants that inform business strategy.

The x-axis shows the growth of the business from left to right as it goes from Entrepreneurial to Preemptive. The y-axis describes our relationship with our clients beginning as strangers and moving up to symbiotic partners. Symbiosis happens in the fourth quadrant (the Winners' Quadrant).

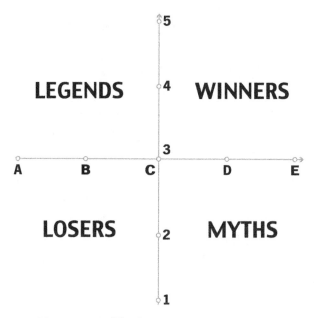

Figure 11.2. The Business Strategy Matrix

Upper Right Quadrant (Winners)

This is the ideal situation: both client and supplier have high ideals, and both are mature enough to work together to achieve these ideals sustainably for the long term. Their shared values and integrated vision enable them to grow together.

As the supplier, you have formed strategic relationships with your best clients, enabling you to gain proprietary insights into their businesses. We might be living in one of the most uncertain economies that has ever existed. Change comes suddenly, without warning. Fortunes can be made and lost overnight. Staying in close, strategic relationships with your clients enables you to have information about your clients that your competitors do not have; you can now use this information, along with your preferential relationships, to collaborate and develop products and services that anticipate what your clients will need to face their emerging challenges.

It's important to note that you are not looking for leadership from your client. You are looking for opportunities to lead your client. While they may be asking for faster horses, you understand them well enough to know that what they really need is a reliable transportation in a changing environment. You can allocate your resources to developing products to fill emerging needs in a changing world. You are constantly in position to make the next best strategic move based on real insight. You constantly redefine the rules of the game. Your competition has no choice but to learn the rules of the new game. Competitors are constantly in catch-up mode.

Your clients are willing to pay for your offerings because they know you are addressing their emerging and strategic needs, and there is a reciprocal understanding of the financial needs of each partner. The client knows that you need to be profitable and enjoys your success, as your success leads to their success. Both you and your best clients understand this interdependence.

Achieving this position and maintaining it depends on your ability to continue to make the right strategic moves. This in turn depends on your ability to maintain strategic relationships with your best clients. You must continually strive to move upward and to the right. Over time, strategic move by strategic move, you will gain momentum and distance yourself from competitors.

Remember this quadrant is not about companies; it's about their strategic moves. The moment a company begins to believe its own press, it will slip out of this quadrant. Value keeps shifting. Companies can only stay in this quadrant by making the right strategic moves.

One of our clients, Mike George, is the CEO of Trisura Guarantee Insurance Company, a Canadian-based Property and Casualty insurance company. Trisura is committed to building strategic relationships with carefully chosen, right-fit customers. The proof of the effectiveness of his strategy is in the numbers. While the overall market is declining, his firm is attracting top talent and enjoying phenomenal year-over-year growth. In fact, in the three years we've been working with him, we've watched his business double. Trisura is agile and is able to make the right moves because of the deep client insights it has.

Lower Left Quadrant (Losers)

In this quadrant, clients and enterprises are at their lowest level of maturity. They are like two needy people coming together simply to get whatever they can get. Clients resent your profitability, and they are constantly trying to drive down the price of your products or services. They compare you to competitors and don't see an advantage to doing business with your firm. They are buying strictly on price, and if another firm has a faster product or the same quality for a few cents less, they will defect.

This is an expensive business model because you are still in the entrepreneurial stage and adjusting your product to each client, but your clients are only shopping on price and trying to drive your price down. The client is unwilling to pay for the individualized service that your business offers, but your business has not grown to the point where it can take advantage of systems and economies of scale. You also have the financial burden of employees without the benefit of systems and processes.

Upper Left Quadrant (Legends)

Here both client and enterprise have high ideals, but one or both don't have the maturity to execute these ideals in the long term. Here your business has a strategic value to your best clients. The clients are willing to pay for the service or goods you provide because they see them as a good fit for their business. You have not yet developed your business to the point that you are able to take full advantage of economies of scale or systems. But there's an even bigger problem. Legends build their businesses around a single idea. They are not businesses that evolve. They are businesses that have one winning formula, and when the formula is rendered irrelevant, as it eventually will be, they are unable to adapt.

An example is a firm that provides training for a particular product, a Microsoft office application. The business is doing very well because clients see the value and appreciate the training provided, but it is a one-trick pony that relies on the delivery of one service. What if Google Apps and Web-based collaboration matures and outstrips Microsoft

Office? What if the desktop becomes obsolete and irrelevant? What if office applications become so simple training isn't required? The next generation in the workplace won't recognize the need for a business that trains users on desktop applications. Think of International Typewriter. When was the last time you thought of the need for training in how to operate a typewriter?

Legends define their perfect client as "someone with a checkbook." They are focused on enhancing and selling their product; therefore they have an eclectic client mix, and if they do develop a new product, it will be a good fit for some clients but not have any applications for others. They need to learn to leverage their strategic relationships to move to the right on the x-axis. They need to have a more focused and effective client-acquisition process so that the cost of developing a new product or service can be shared over their entire client base and used to solve problems repeatedly.

Bottom Right Quadrant (Myths)

These are larger companies that seem successful on the surface because of performance in the past. However, when you drill down, you find they are empty. Clients are there because of some form of coercion. It's like the relationship where all appearances of success are there, but the relationship is dysfunctional in nature—one dominates and one is trapped.

I have been with the same cell phone supplier for over a decade. This is not by choice. Every time I upgrade to a new device, I am forced into a three-year agreement. Somehow, magically, just before the end of the three-year term they come out with some new gadget that I feel will be an advantage to me, and they force me to sign another three-year agreement to obtain the new product.

They continue to daisy chain a series of handcuffs that maintains me as their client. I am a captive customer, not a loyal customer. The services my supplier provides are all right, but I am not really delighted. I make sacrifices. For example, I have to accept that I will often lose calls in the rural area where I live. If I was on a month-to-month agreement and remained with my supplier for over ten years by choice, that would be a true indication of the value I receive from them.

Are you working for a big firm with captive customers? Do these customers really value you, or would they desert you if your artificial fence came down and they were given a choice? If the latter, you are working for a myth. Myths will eventually die. Their cash reserves and captive customers buy them time to figure out how to get back in the Winners' Quadrant.

Often the firms in this quadrant are big companies run by individuals with big egos. They have achieved a level of preeminence, which makes it difficult to "speak truth to power."

Conclusion

Our world has changed dramatically. Past changes are leading to more dramatic and even faster change. Overnight success is no longer inconceivable. Neither is overnight demise. Agility is one of the key attributes required for success today. That agility, however, must be in the context of an authentic identity and a genuine commitment to help others realize their heartfelt visions. This combination of authentic identity, genuine commitment to service, and strategic agility is what will propel you and keep you in the Winners' Quadrant.

Essentially, to succeed today we must build human-to-human enterprises. We must acknowledge the special, creative powers that exist in all our "human resources." We must understand that people want to express their highest natures. They will do so only when they are in service to other people who are seeking to express their highest natures. In the end, human-to-human selling is not selling at all. It is the process of creating a better planet for everyone who lives here.

CEO Action Plan

- ☐ Figure out what quadrant your company is currently in.
- ☐ Build a game plan for moving into and staying in the Winners' Quadrant based on focusing on right-fit customers.

Sales Professional Action Plan

- ☐ Commit to having strategic conversations with your customers to gain insight on where they are going and how their world is changing.
- ☐ Speak up. Let your senior management team know you have a perspective. Be the advocate for your right-fit clients.
- ☐ Learn to balance what you ask for with what you give. If you are giving great value to your employer in terms of profitable sales, you earn the right to be heard.
- ☐ Never whine. Realize resources are scarce. Always see the cup as half full and search for positive solutions to every challenge.

Chapter 13

THE WAY FORWARD

You can judge your age by the amount of pain you feel when you come in contact with a new idea.
—Pearl S. Buck

In the end, what goes around comes around. We can choose to live in the negative cycle of supplier sabotage and buyer backlash, or we can choose to engage in human-to-human selling and create cycles of symbiosis. With the promise of design thinking, there are certainly ways to create enterprise symbiosis from the top down. But I believe there's great promise in starting from the ground up: through the sales department. If you're a salesperson focusing on developing human-to-human relationships rather than taking a short-term or adversarial approach, you'll not only model the process of symbiosis for your enterprise, you just might love your job again.

The truth is no matter where we find ourselves in the company hierarchy, we have responsibilities as both buyers and sellers in this new world of commerce.

As buyers:

- Let's not look for the lowest price. Let's look for the best solution.
- Let's look for partners who can deliver real value.
- Let's think long-term rather than short-term.
- Let's think of mutual gain rather than exclusive gain.
- Let's allow our suppliers to make money when working with us.

Remember the old adage, "One good turn deserves another." Let's make it clear to our suppliers that we'll honor their prices, but we expect them to honor our expectations.

As sellers:

- Let's focus on delivering real value to our customers who put their trust in us, and let's commit to helping them achieve their desired outcomes, not just delivering a product or service.
- Let's see our buyers as human beings who are trying to aspire to or achieve something, not just people who buy our stuff.
- Let's ensure we understand the outcomes our buyers are searching for.
- Let's commit to helping them achieve their desired outcomes, and let's stay with them until they do.

This is the only way we will build a sustainable economy and a world that we'll enjoy living in.

ABOUT THE AUTHOR

For over twenty years, Adrian Davis has been devoted to understanding and applying the principles of successful selling in business. Adrian holds a Bachelor of Business Administration from the University of Ottawa (Dean's Honor List). He is also a certified Competitive Intelligence Professional (CIP) and a certified Professional in Business Process Management (P.BPM).

In 2002, Adrian founded Whetstone Inc., a sales training and consulting firm specializing in helping businesses dramatically grow their revenues.

Adrian is a sought-after, world-class professional speaker and is frequently called upon to advise senior management teams and sales groups on the subjects of sales and corporate strategy, relationship management, and sales excellence.

Access free training on human-to-human selling at: http:// adriandavis.com/Free-Resources.

Resources

Would you like to connect with others who are committed to human-to-human selling? If you'd like to share your own experiences, learn from others, and gain access to deeper resources from Adrian Davis and Whetstone Inc., join our free online community at http://adriandavis.com/Free-Resources.

Templates mentioned in the book that are available in our community center:

1. Free training course
2. Relationship assessment scorecard
3. Question library
4. Cost justification worksheet
5. Account strategy
6. Storytelling template